Essentials of Discussion and Debate

ESSENTIALS OF

AND

DISCUSSION

DEBATE

By **HALBERT E. GULLEY**
University of Illinois

Holt, Rinehart and Winston   *New York*
Chicago   ·   San Francisco   ·   Toronto
London

Preface

This handbook is written for the student who is participating in discussion and debate, either in high school or college, in the classroom or as an extraclass activity. It attempts to explain, as concisely as possible, the *essential* theory and procedure involved. The person who would use these processes wisely must understand them. The purpose of this book is to enhance the value of participation as meaningful contribution to democratic decision-making.

Training in discussion and debate is training in self-government. For people to govern themselves, they must be free (1) to inquire, to find out, to know the facts; (2) to express reasoned convictions, and to hear those of others; and (3) to choose among alternatives. In discussion we define, investigate, explore, inquire, listen to others, weigh all possibilities, evaluate alternatives, and choose a plan of action. While evaluating, however, honest differences of opinion arise. It is proper and reasonable, then, to debate. In debate we explain and advocate what is to us the soundest proposal. After careful discussion and sincere advocacy, when each person has had a courteous hearing, we can proceed to choose a policy which will (1) satisfy everyone or (2) fulfill the wishes of the majority.

Rational discussion and reasoned advocacy *both* contribute to the soundness of a group decision. Without objective inquiry, some facts may be concealed from the group, and sensible alternatives may be overlooked. In considering many problems, moreover, the absence of opportunity for sincere debate may lead the group to adopt an inferior course of action through failure to consider fully its limitations and the advantages of other possibilities, or may cause some persons to feel their proposal has not had a fair hearing. Both discussion and debate, then, are reasonable, justifiable processes and, in many cases, both are *essential* to rational group deliberation.

At the same time, it must be realized that discussion and debate are not *ends in themselves.* They are *means* by which people with a problem proceed sensibly toward a solution. The *decision,* what to do, is the end product. Discussion and debate, in schools or anywhere, make little sense as games, or entertainment, or ends in themselves. But as activities which provide practice in the basic processes of democratic decision-making, they are among the most valuable subjects one can study.

It is hoped that this book may contribute to the student's understanding of deliberation so that he can place his participation in proper perspective as part of a much larger democratic procedure. A further hope is that the theory presented here may make him a more effective participant. The book can be used as a reference work by the high school or college student who wants to participate in discussion and debate but who has had little or no instruction in argumentation or group process. The experienced discusser and debater should find it helpful as a guide for reviewing the principles of sound preparation and performance. The book also can be used as a text-book in high school courses in discussion and debate, or in speech or English courses which feature a unit of instruction on one or both of these subjects.

H. E. G.

Urbana, Illinois
January 1955

Contents

Preface · v

1 Definitions and Relationships · 1
2 Questions and Propositions · 11
3 Finding the Facts · 19
4 Inference, Reason, and Support · 29

Discussion

5 Types of Discussion · 51
6 Preparing for Discussion · 59
7 Participating in Discussion · 67
8 Leading Discussion · 77
9 Evaluating Discussion · 85

Debate

10 Types of Debate · 89
11 Preparing for Debate · 97
12 Refutation and Rebuttal · 115
13 Presentation · 124
14 Evaluating Debate · 133
15 Ethics in Deliberation · 138

Index · 141

Essentials of Discussion and Debate

1

Definitions and Relationships

The crucial distinction between a free nation and a dictatorship is freedom to discuss and debate proposals for change. When we can speak out against our leaders, pass resolutions designed to influence governmental policy, tell our elected representatives how we think they should vote, and remove them if they displease us, we live in a free society. Persons living in an authoritarian state can only acquiesce silently in decisions of their rulers or suffer the consequences of disagreement.

To control and preserve a democratic society, citizens must know how to use these privileges. We must be proficient in studying problems, examining policies, and stating convictions. In other words, we must be proficient in discussion and debate.

These are the procedures which occupy a group in moving from a problem to a decision. This whole process we call *deliberation*.

EMERGENCE OF PROBLEMS

Man is never without problems. Some are personal: Where will we get money for college tuition? How shall we choose our dates or mates? The school, too, has problems. How can teachers help students learn more? What courses should be required? Should students be given more self-government? On wider horizons, difficulties are even more complex. There are political, social, and economic problems at every level of organization: community, state, national, and international. How can the civic club serve our city? Who is the best candidate for Governor? Should education remain the responsibility of the states? Is there too much centralization of power in Washington? How can the United States best contribute to world peace? To list all the problems in which we are involved in our home, school, city, clubs, church, future vocation or business, state, region, and nation would require a catalog of impressive size and complexity.

How do these difficulties emerge into pressing questions requiring discussion and debate? Some arise out of specific events or changes and require an immediate decision. The head of a school dies or retires, for example, and the governing board must choose a successor. In their meeting, board members discuss the relative merits of applicants. If there is strong disagreement, debate may ensue, with individuals advocating their particular choice. The decision may be made at the end of the meeting by general agreement (called *consensus*) or by majority vote.

Many complex problems, however, do not arise suddenly, but develop slowly. Take juvenile delinquency, for instance. The first signs of difficulty may be reports of isolated cases. Two youths are arrested for stealing hubcaps from parked automobiles. Police complain that teenagers are holding noisy demonstrations downtown late at night. Boys from a near-by town invade the city and throw rocks at young people in front of a drugstore. At this point, parents may appear before the city council and ask what is being done to prevent these acts. Members of women's clubs, civic organizations, churches, and school boards may meet to discuss them. The newspaper may print an editorial recommending a city-financed youth center to keep boys and girls off the streets. Other people may suggest remedies.

The problem will be a matter for discussion and debate in many different groups in the city. The nature of their deliberation will depend on (1) the particular group's *power to act;* and (2) the extent of agreement within the group. Keep in mind that each group begins initially with a statement of the problem and moves toward a decision, what to do.

THE DELIBERATION CONTINUUM

The process of moving from a problem to a decision may be thought of as a deliberative continuum, or a continuous progression of closely related steps. Discussion comes first, and involves these stages: (1) stating the problem; (2) defining what is meant by the terms used in stating the problem; (3) analyzing the difficulty by considering the facts relevant to the history and nature of the problem; (4) suggesting possible remedies or alternative courses of action for moving toward a solution; (5) evaluating these alternatives by weighing the advantages and disadvantages of each possible course of action; and (6) choosing the best course of action.

Deliberation may end here (1) if the group can agree; and (2) if it has final authority to act. Where the group cannot agree or must recommend action to a larger body for final decision, the deliberation process will assume different forms, as the following descriptions indicate.

Deliberation 1: Group agrees after discussion, has power to act

The city council may discuss juvenile delinquency, weigh possible remedies, and decide to build a city youth center. A church group may meet and discuss what that particular church could do to lessen juvenile problems. If the group agrees on an action to take, their deliberation ends, since they have power to decide what their organization can do.

A diagram of this kind of deliberation would probably look like this:

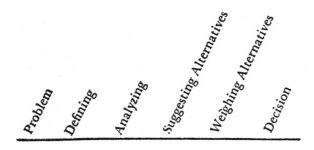

→ DISCUSSION

Deliberation 2: Group agrees after discussion, does not have power to act

If the group can agree, but does not have power to act on its decision, then the deliberation diagram will be just the same as in Deliberation One, except that the end product, decision, will constitute a *recommendation* for action. Suppose the church group discusses, not what that church can do, but what the city council should do to curb juvenile delinquency. Their recommendation, arrived at through discussion, will go to the city council where it will be subjected to further deliberation.

Much of the deliberation in a democratic society on political, economic, and social problems is of this type. All kinds of groups decide what they think should be United States foreign policy, for example, and submit their recommendations to their elected officials. When student groups discuss, "How can the United States best combat the influences of communism?" they are *recommendation groups.* The combined influences of all the groups and individuals making up our democratic society determine what governmental policy will be.

Deliberation 3: Group disagrees after discussion, has power to act

What if the group cannot agree after discussion? Then debate follows discussion. Suppose two of the six members of the city council want to build a youth center, two favor stricter laws as a remedy, and two fail to see the necessity for any action. The matter may be dropped for the moment, but if the citizenry is insisting on action, it must be taken up again. At the next meeting, the advocates of each position may present reasoned arguments, backed by evidence, for following the plan of action they favor. Two members speak for a youth center, two for stricter laws, and two for doing nothing. Perhaps some citizens may attend the meeting and make speeches of advocacy from the floor. After the debate, the council must still make a decision. Again, they can reach this decision by general agreement or majority vote. Before deciding, they may once more go back to discussion; they may redefine, re-analyze, and re-evaluate alternatives.

The whole deliberation in this situation can be diagramed this way:

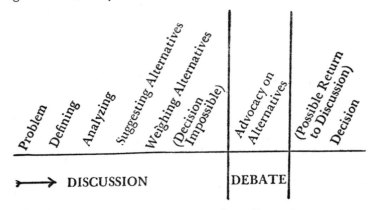

Deliberation 4: Group disagrees after discussion, does not have power to act

If the group disagrees after discussion, debate follows, as in the diagram for Deliberation Three. Where the group does not have power to act, however, the decision reached is again a *recommendation,* as was the case in Deliberation Two.

In the church group, for example, debate could have followed discussion if disagreement had developed. After members had advocated their proposals, the group would have decided what it wanted to recommend to the city council.

APPLICATION TO COMPLEX SITUATIONS

In two of these four deliberative situations, there is a recommendation to a larger group responsible for the final decision. This outcome leads to a multiplication of the occasions for discussion and debate, but the basic processes involved remain the same.

Using again the example of the city council, suppose the council agrees that the best solution is to build a youth center, but that the city has no funds for the purpose. The council may propose financing the center through a bond issue, which needs the approval of the people at a special election. The council would make its recommendation to the voters at the end of discussion, and perhaps debate, as diagramed in Deliberation Two or Deliberation Four. Between the time of the council's recommendation and the special election, more discussion and debate takes place in all kinds of organizations and meetings. Debate is particularly important in this period, because we now have a specific proposition, Resolved: That the city should issue bonds to finance a youth center. City councilmen may speak in a public debate as advocates of the bond issue. The final decision is then made by the voters. To diagram the deliberation continuum in this case, let's assume the council's recommendation resulted from Deliberation Four:

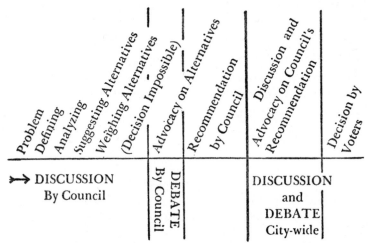

There are many situations in which complex deliberation occurs. A committee of a legislature, for example, deliberates and reaches a recommendation through discussion—or both discussion and debate. When the recommendation reaches the floor of the assembly, it is debated by the whole membership and the final decision comes from voting. We elect the President of the United States in this same way. The *recommendation groups* in this case are the nominating conventions of the political parties. Through deliberation, including debate, they recommend candidates to the people. The merits of the candidates are then debated by the whole nation until election day. Decision is reached at the ballot box.

DEFINITIONS

These possibilities suggest the complex nature of deliberation in a society where people govern themselves. We now can see what groups are doing when they discuss and when they debate, and when they are doing one and when the other.

Discussion defined

Discussion takes place when a cooperating group states, defines, and analyzes a problem, suggests and evaluates possible solutions, and attempts to reach a decision which will be acceptable to all or to the majority.[1]

---

[1] There is another kind of discussion which we will encounter later in considering types of discussion (see Chapter 5). The definition given here is for problem-solving discussion as a part of deliberation. The other broad purpose for which discussion may be employed is that of self-enlightenment or study, where the outcomes are sharing of ideas and fuller understanding.

Debate defined

When disagreement develops over a particular remedy, debate may occur. Debate also occurs when advocates and opponents of a recommended action try to influence a decision of persons with final power to act. Debate is reasoned advocacy, for or against a proposal, where each speaker attempts to convince others that his suggestions should be accepted.

The deliberator must recognize the implications of these definitions:

1. The advocate must realize that debate is only a section from the middle of the deliberation continuum. After debaters have had a fair hearing, they must work with the group to reach a decision. When student debaters engage in an interscholastic contest, they should recognize that their performance is not an end in itself. A particular debate has training value for the participant, but it has greater significance as part of a much larger deliberation where the citizens of a whole nation are striving to solve a vital political, economic, or social problem.

2. The person who enjoys discussion but is critical of debate must understand that *both* discussion and debate are functional parts of the deliberative process. Without debate we could not reach decisions in many situations. Since disagreement is normal, we must allow debate as a means of resolving differences; otherwise, men resort to violence and war as a means of decision-making.

3. The *same person* is a discusser and a debater at different moments and in different situations. We hope he is just as honest and sincere in one situation as the other.

EXERCISES

1. (a) Make a list of the *problems* which you face in each of the following situations. Word each problem as a question.
   (1) As a member of a family group
   (2) As a student in the school
   (3) As a citizen of your community
   (4) As a citizen of your state
   (5) As a citizen of the United States.
   (b) Examine this list of problems and classify them into three categories:
   (1) Those which must be decided by you alone
   (2) Those which will probably be decided by group deliberation without debate
   (3) Those which will probably be decided by group deliberation, including debate.
2. Trace the history of the development of a controversy in your school or community from its earliest manifestations to its emergence as a question for discussion and debate.
3. Visit some local deliberative assembly, such as a meeting of your student governing body or city council. While the meeting is in progress, keep a running commentary of the stages of deliberation. Write a report which describes the stages of defining, analyzing, weighing alternatives, advocating, and so on. Include in your written report a continuum showing the chronological sequence of discussion and/or debate. Note that the group in a single meeting may go through the stages of discussion and advocacy more than once, even on the same problem. You may also observe deliberation which consists only of debate, without preliminary discussion.
4. Listen to a discussion program broadcast by radio or television. Following closely the definitions presented in this chapter, decide whether the program you hear is discussion or debate or a combination of both.

2

Questions and Propositions

Discussion begins with a problem worded as a question: What, if anything, should our city do to lessen juvenile delinquency? This query is one of *policy;* i.e., it asks what future action ought to be taken in the best interests of everyone concerned. There are two other types. A question of *fact* deals with the truth or falsity of a condition or event, past or present. An example is: Are the taverns in our city selling liquor to minors? A third type is one of *value,* which involves an evaluation or judgment: Are Saturday night dances a good influence on youngsters?

We usually discuss problems of *policy,* since matters requiring group deliberation most often involve the desirability of some future course of action. In considering a larger problem of future policy, however, we discuss at various times during the deliberation subquestions of *fact* and *value.* In the examples given above, "What, if anything, should our city do to lessen juvenile delinquency?" would be the larger deliberation. While analyzing the problem, we would inquire into the causes. Here we would ask questions of fact: Are the taverns in our city selling liquor to minors? Are juveniles loitering on the city streets late at night? Is the crime rate among youths in our city increasing? The response we want is a specific representation of the situation as it exists or existed. On the matter of loitering, we must know, for example, how many youngsters of what ages are seen on the city streets at what hours.

Questions of value also become subquestions in any discussion of policy. While considering possible solutions to delinquency, someone might propose community-sponsored Saturday night dances for young people. We then ask a question of value: Are Saturday night dances a good influence on youngsters? Here we must respond both with facts and opinions. Judgment involves an individual's personal concepts, attitudes, and religious beliefs, but his evaluation should be based on careful consideration of relevant facts.

We saw in Chapter 1 that debate propositions emerge from the discussion stage of deliberation. If disagreement develops about Saturday night dances as a solution to delinquency, this proposal can become a subject for debate. The proposition may again be one of *policy, value,* or *fact.*

If the proposal is to inaugurate such a program, the proposition would be one of future *policy,* Resolved: That our city should sponsor Saturday night dances for young people. We would debate the desirability of this course of action. If our judgments conflict, the proposition could be one of *value,* Resolved: That Saturday night dances are a good influence on youngsters. Here again the matter of values might become a subproposition to be considered while debating the larger question of policy.

You have noticed the similarity of discussion questions and debate propositions up to this point. The proposition of *fact,* however, is not quite the same as the question of fact in discussion. We should not debate matters which can be settled by doing research. The question: Are juveniles loitering on the city streets late at night? is a sensible question to ask and answer in the early stages of discussion. But we shouldn't debate it when we can survey the situation and find out. The proposition of fact in debate is ordinarily reserved for matters in which the true situation which exists or existed is not easily verifiable. Law courts furnish the best examples. In a murder trial the proposition is, Resolved: That X murdered Y on the night of January 16. The prosecuting attorney affirms, the defense lawyer denies.

Propositions of fact are sometimes important outside the courtroom, of course, when the facts are subject to dispute. In complex matters such as standard of living, for instance, we might debate, Resolved: That the farmer has a higher standard of living now than before the war. The proposition is one of fact, indeed, but it is of a much higher order of complexity than the discussion questions of fact we have been citing. It involves what is meant by "standard of living," which in turn requires a judgment and takes us at least partially out of the realm of "facts."

REQUIREMENTS FOR A DISCUSSION QUESTION

A discussion question must meet certain standards of limitation, appropriateness, and wording. Although the participant often finds the question already worked out by someone else before he begins his preparation, he can benefit from understanding the requirements for a good question. He then can help a group word subquestions which can be adequately covered in each phase of the discussion.

1. It should deal with a single problem. Only confusion

can result if a group attempts to talk about two or more problems at the same time.

2. It should be limited in scope to the time available. The question, "What can be done to secure peace in the world?" obviously cannot be covered in a one-hour discussion. Worded in this general way it can never be fully discussed. Proper limitation will improve the quality of the discussion and avoid frustration. A more specific problem is: "What should the United Nations do to settle peaceably the Arab refugee problem?" This question has been limited in two ways: (a) it asks what a single agency, the U.N., can do; and (b) it confines consideration to a particular aspect of the world peace problem. However, worded in this way, it still may be too broad for a short discussion.

3. The question should be appropriate to the participants. It should interest the group, and should concern matters in which they are competent or can become competent through study. It should be drawn from an area in which the group has power to act or to influence; i.e., the outcome of their deliberation should make a difference. Students can profitably discuss United States foreign policy because as citizens they can combine with others to influence the conduct of our government. It would be pointless for them to discuss what should be the foreign policy of Russia since they cannot influence it.

4. It should be carefully worded as a *question*. It should not contain ambiguous terms. The question, "Should subversive teachers be penalized?" is not satisfactory, since the meanings of "subversive" and "penalized" are not clear. The group will wrangle immediately about what is meant. To make clear what the group is to decide, a wording such

as this would be better: "Should teachers who are members of the Communist Party be allowed to teach?" The question also should be worded impartially; it should not show any bias for a particular point of view. In the question: "Should the ridiculous game of football be abolished?" the wording suggests a judgment before the group begins discussion.

REQUIREMENTS FOR A DEBATE PROPOSITION

A debate proposition also should meet certain standards. The debater should know these requirements not only because he often needs to help word a proposition for special occasions when a national debate topic is not being used, but also because such understanding helps him recognize weaknesses in propositions worded for him. Like the discussion question, the debate proposition should deal with a single problem, be limited to the time available, and be appropriate to the participants. In addition:

1. It should be debatable. It must involve a controversy in which honest differences of opinion arise, and which is subject to substantial proof on either side. It must not be a matter which can be resolved through simple research.

2. It should be carefully worded as a declarative statement. It should not contain ambiguous terms and should be stated as concisely as possible.

3. A proposition of policy usually should declare that a change ought to be made in existing policy. Traditionally, the first speaker in a debate represents the affirmative team. When the topic advocates a change from the present system, the affirmative has the burden of proving that the change should be made. Thus, the basis for the controversy immediately becomes clear during the first speech. The

proposition should read, Resolved: That the United States should nationalize the steel industry; rather than, Resolved: That the steel industry in the United States should remain in private hands.

EXERCISES

1. Find newspaper editorials supporting the three types of propositions: fact, value, and policy. Write a report in which you state the three propositions, if they are not explicitly stated in the editorials, and evaluate the propositions according to the requirements presented in this chapter.

2. (a) Apply the tests of a satisfactory discussion question to the following proposed topics:
   (1) Should Italy recognize the Communist Government of China?
   (2) Should world armaments be reduced?
   (3) Should the United States adopt a program of compulsory national health insurance and subsidize the training of additional doctors of medicine?
   (4) How can education be improved?
   (5) To what extent should the government reduce the unfair and unwise farm subsidy program?
   (b) Reword those questions you consider unsatisfactory.

3. (a) Apply the tests of a satisfactory debate proposition to the following proposed resolutions:
   (1) Resolved: That the pernicious custom of voting a straight political ticket should be abandoned.
   (2) Resolved: That the United States should nationalize and prohibit strikes in the coal mines of the nation.
   (3) Resolved: That the present method of electing the President of the United States should be retained.
   (4) Resolved: That there are more Democrats than Republicans in this state.
   (5) Resolved: That a liberal education which broadens students and makes them aware of the cul-

tural influences of their heritage is superior to training which prepares the student for his life work.

(b) Reword those propositions you consider unsatisfactory.

3

Finding the Facts

Occasionally the director of forensics overhears such remarks as this: "Oh, are we going to have a discussion? Is that where people just sit around and talk?" Or he may hear this: "I don't know much about that subject but I sure enjoy arguing about it." The students who make these statements are implying that they can discuss and debate without being well informed about the problem. No notion could be further from the truth. Deliberation based on ignorance or inaccurate information can hardly be dignified by the name. A pleasing voice cannot make a success of communication if the message is devoid of meaningful content. Audiences and discussion participants are impatient with speakers who talk without saying anything. They are even more disturbed by communicators who distort, present "facts" which just simply are not true, or are unable to explain the source of their information.

The deliberator must make a special effort to know the facts. He must be doubly certain that his information is accurate in every detail and that his sources are reliable.

SYSTEMATIC APPROACH

In order to know a subject thoroughly, you as a deliberator must search diligently for information. You must not be satisfied with material furnished by an industrious colleague or any other single source. Investigate every fund of information available to you.

To search intelligently, you must have a general idea of the kinds of facts you are seeking. Much time will be wasted if you wander aimlessly through magazines and books looking for material. Make your search purposeful. Also, be generous in your research, even to the extent of collecting more material than you ultimately may use.

Develop a systematic method of classifying the information you find. If you were studying the problem of free trade, for example, you could have a category for evidence of "increasing domestic production" and another for "increasing American exports." When you locate material on these matters, take careful notes on 3 by 5 cards, or some other cards or sheets of uniform size. On each separate card you should record three kinds of information:

1. An identification of the category of information to which this piece of evidence belongs, such as "increasing domestic production."
2. A complete citation of the source in which the information was found, including full name of author, title of magazine or book, date of publication, and pages.
3. An accurate quotation of the pertinent remarks, or a paraphrase of the contents (the author's exact meaning written in your own words). When quoting directly, be sure to put quotation marks around the words of the author so you will not wonder later whether the words are yours or his.

A single card may contain more than one fact without becoming a source of confusion to you later provided that all the information on the card relates to the same category:

Beatrice P. Lamb,   High U. S. Tariffs
"Trade—And Aid," Public
Affairs Pamphlet No. 195,
1953, p. 17.

"There are still many articles on which prohibitively high tariff rates prevail."

Product	U. S. Tariff Rate
Most kinds of lace	90%
Imitation pearls	90%
Perfumes	over 100%
Most toys	70%

In the process of doing research on the problem of free trade, you could collect hundreds of cards similar to this one. If each one is carefully identified by its category in the upper right-hand corner, it is an easy matter to sort out all the evidence you have on "high U. S. tariffs" simply by assembling all the cards labeled in this way.

LOCATING FACTS

Each of the following sources should be investigated for any possible material relevant to the discussion or debate topic. Obviously, all will not furnish facts for every subject. You will be wise, however, to gather information from as many different sources as you can.

1. *Recall your personal experiences.* Many students

assume they have had no personal experience which would be of use in deliberation. For some questions, this assumption may be valid. In many instances, however, you have been personally involved in situations which are relevant. When considering fair employment practices, for example, you may discover that you have known persons who were denied employment because of race, color, or creed, and you may be familiar with the employment practices of some firms. Your contributions will be much more lively and convincing if you report such experiences.

The first step in research, then, is to set down in writing, preferably on cards of the type described, whatever personal experience you have had with the subject.

2. *Go and see.* Another common misconception held by many is that information must come almost wholly from what is printed in books. Although no one should underestimate the importance of printed materials, you can profitably supplement your reading on many topics through personal observation. If the topic is federal aid to education, you can visit schools and observe conditions for yourself.

There are three requirements for observing and reporting observations in a satisfactory manner. The first is *seeing accurately.* You must place yourself in a position from which you can observe. You must spend sufficient time on the scene to see what is there. Another essential is *reporting accurately.* This requisite involves exact use of words. You must be able to put into words precisely what you observed, so listeners who did not see will understand exactly what you witnessed. A third requirement is *reporting fairly.* You must attempt to describe what you saw without regard to whether you *like* what you observed. If you personally oppose federal aid to education because you feel our schools are at present satisfactory, you must be careful not to make your report on schools sound more favorable than the conditions warrant. After you have reported the situation fairly, you are free to draw conclusions from these facts which will introduce your own opinion as to what should be done.

3. Talk with someone who knows. A superintendent of schools may give you valuable information about federal aid to education. He can also give you his *opinion* about the need for aid and the possibility of federal control. Interviewing those who are well informed will give you many ideas for further research and will contribute to your grasp of the subject, so long as you choose persons competent in their fields and do not depend wholly upon one person.

Before talking with busy people, arrange for an interview at their convenience. They will be happy to talk with you if you approach them properly. Plan carefully what you want to ask. Don't waste their time with trivialities or ask them for information available in books.

4. Listen and read. A fourth source of information is readily available in the form of radio and television programs and current newspapers and magazines. Listen to the discussion programs on radio and television every week. Make it a point to hear addresses by federal and state officials and other prominent citizens. Read widely in magazines and newspapers as they are delivered to your own home. The discusser and debater should be well informed about current affairs; his preparation should be a constant process. A particularly rewarding habit is to read thoroughly one or two good newspapers every day.

5. *Use the library.* The richest source of facts is that almost unlimited storehouse of ideas—the library.

a. *Books.* In most libraries, books may be located efficiently by consulting a card catalog where they are listed on small cards arranged alphabetically. Usually they are listed in three places: by author's last name, by title, and by subject. If your library does not have a card catalog, the librarian will guide you to books on a particular subject.

b. *Magazines.* The most valuable general index to magazine articles is the *Readers' Guide to Periodical Literature.* Articles are indexed by author's name and by subjects. In addition to *Readers' Guide* most libraries provide indexes on special subjects such as *Education Index, Agricultural Index,* etc.

c. *Newspapers.* Some school libraries and many public libraries maintain collections of newspapers. The only extensive index to such material in this country is the *New York Times Index.* If your library has this index and a file of the *New York Times,* you will find it helpful in locating reports of past events as well as opinion in columns and editorials. The *New York Times Index* is also helpful as a guide to materials appearing on the same days in newspapers other than the *Times.*

d. *Pamphlets.* Pamphlets sometimes offer material which is difficult to find elsewhere. Two indexes of such publications are the H. W. Wilson *Vertical File Service* and the *Public Affairs Information Service.*

Pamphlets published by special interest groups can usually be purchased for a nominal amount by writing to the organization (such as the American Federation of Labor, Congress of Industrial Organization, National Association of Manufacturers). Addresses of these and similar groups and the cost of each pamphlet are listed in these two indexes. Often the pamphlets are provided free of charge.

It is necessary to remember when using such publications that the material contained there usually reflects the views of the group which had them printed.

e. *Encyclopedias.* Information of a general nature may be found in such encyclopedias as the *Britannica* and the *Americana.* Such sources are worth while as a beginning point in library research. Articles are usually written by an expert on the subject and often list other works which may be consulted. Encyclopedias devoted to special fields, such as the *Encyclopedia of the Social Sciences,* also are available.

f. *Biographies.* Information on persons cited as authorities in discussion and debate may be located in *Who's Who in America* and the *Dictionary of American Biography.* British equivalents are *Who's Who* and *Dictionary of National Biography.* There are also specialized biographies for men in education, business, and other fields, and for geographical areas, such as *Who's Who in the Midwest.*

g. *Statistical information.* Much exact information may be obtained from the *World Almanac, Information Please Almanac, Statesman's Yearbook, Statistical Abstract of the United States,* and similar sources.

h. *Government publications.* The discusser and debater will find much valuable material in the *Congressional Record,* a report of the speeches in Congress, plus an appendix containing additional remarks, editorials reprinted from newspapers, and other kinds of information. Reports of the hearings of Congressional committees, and publications of governmental departments such as the Department of Commerce, are also fertile sources.

TESTING SOURCES

Some of the information you locate may be inaccurate or biased. Much material is printed and many opinions are spoken by persons who have "axes to grind." To be an intelligent reader and listener, you must be able to evaluate sources. You can test sources by asking questions such as these:

1. Does this source have a reputation for accuracy? Does this newspaper print the facts about events exactly as they occurred? Are the facts printed in this magazine verified by reports from other sources? Has the author of this book checked his facts with care?

2. Is this source prejudiced? Does this person distort the facts to fit his preconceived ideas? Does this magazine present only one side of a controversy? Does this newspaper "color" the news by printing those items favorable to a particular set of interests or political party? Has the man I interviewed shown a bias because of the company for which he works or the causes in which he believes?

3. Is this information recent? Are the facts presented in this source out of date? Were they true last year or last month but not today?

4. Is this information complete? Am I given all the facts? Are some facts being withheld? Have I checked every possible source of information?

Careful questioning of sources in this manner will lead to more accurate and stimulating discussion and debate. It will also demonstrate the wisdom of basing preparation on more than a single source of information. If you will interview two or more experts, instead of one, and read two or more books, newspapers, or magazines, you will be more likely to obtain a true picture of the facts as they really exist. By relying on a single source, you can easily be misled and misinformed, and thereby misinform and mislead others. Your error will be further multiplied if this single source is unreliable, prejudiced, out of date, or incomplete.

EXERCISES

1. Hand to your instructor ten model note cards showing source, classification, and information as suggested in this chapter.
2. Interview one of your colleagues, questioning him in detail on a subject on which he feels thoroughly informed. Write a report of what you learned from his answers. Then show the report to the colleague interviewed and ask him if you have reported his views *accurately* and *fairly*.
3. Draw up a bibliography on one of the current national debate propositions; divide it into sections such as the following: books, magazine articles, pamphlets, government publications, and so on. Within each section, list items alphabetically.
4. Look for reports of the same event in at least two newspapers and two weekly newsmagazines. Compare the four reports carefully. Write a report on any indications you note of inaccuracy, bias, distortion, or lack of completeness. Remember that these tendencies may be unintentional.

4

Inference, Reason, and Support

In deliberation we work with *probability* and not with perfect "Truth." The scientist sometimes can be "positive." The physicist may discover that certain magnets attract iron; he can test and retest this conclusion and it will "always" be so.

We are not so fortunate in considering social, economic, and political problems. Does the United States have a "better" system of medicine than does Britain? Would a federal world government be "better" than the United Nations? We cannot settle these questions in test tubes or laboratories by counting, weighing, or measuring.

We must reason. We must search for evidence which *tends* to make us reach a certain conclusion. Always we must be cautious of our facts, inferences, and conclusions. We can find few identical instances from past experience on which to base a generalization about any form of government. At best, we can conclude that one system is *probably* better than another, or that this action will *probably* avert war. It is a reckless debater, indeed, who asserts he has "conclusively proved" anything. The discusser, of course, is not so tempted to exaggerate his positiveness.

On what basis do we decide what to do? Suppose there is an important dance at the school tomorrow night and you are a boy considering asking your father for the family automobile. Deliberation on the problem will have two phases: (1) your examination of the situation in order to decide whether having the car would benefit you; and (2) your presentation of remarks to your father which will lead him to grant your request.

Let's look at the first phase: will you benefit from having the car? Immediately you go over the conditions which will exist tomorrow night:

The dance starts at 8 o'clock.
It is being held at the school.
Your girl lives 15 blocks from school.
It is 5 blocks from your house to your girl's house.
You get off work at the drugstore at 7 o'clock.
Your girl will wear a formal dress.
The week has been rainy.
Jim Brown and Ron Fuller are taking their girls to the dance in cars.

These items are the *facts* of the situation. By themselves, however, the facts mean little. They take on meaning when we start putting them together and "seeing" their implications. If you have to work until 7 o'clock, eat supper, dress, travel 5 blocks to your girl's house, travel another 15 blocks to school, and arrive in time for an 8 o'clock dance, you are going to have a time problem. How do you know that? You have made an *inference*, which is a mental leap from fact to implication or conclusion. When these facts are put together, they point to an implication which has significance. Looking backward from the inference, the facts are pieces of *evidence* that you will have a shortage of time.

You will draw other inferences from these facts:

Facts: Your girl will wear a formal dress.
              She lives 15 blocks from school.

Inference: It will be difficult for her to walk 15 blocks in a long dress.

Facts: The week has been rainy.
              Your girl will wear a formal dress.

Inference: The sidewalks will probably be wet and her skirt may touch the ground and be ruined.

Facts: Jim Brown and Ron Fuller are taking their girls to the dance in cars.

Inference: You will feel like a "piker" if you ask your girl to walk.

From all these inferences, you reach a still more complex inference: you should probably provide some kind of transportation to the dance. What kinds are possible? Which one would be best? The whole mental process you are going through—examining facts, drawing inferences, seeing implications, considering possibilities—is called *reasoning*. The conclusion you may reach, based on your reasoning, is that you should ask your father for the family car.

Now we're ready for phase two: presenting remarks to your father which will lead him to grant your request. You have reached a conclusion which satisfies you. When you present it to him, and try to show him why this is a reasonable request, you will be presenting *argument*. You will use the same pieces of evidence (fact) already examined to *support* your argument. Your "speech" to him might go something like this:

I need to borrow the family car tomorrow night to take my girl to the dance, because
  There will not be time enough to walk, because
    I have only an hour from the time I finish work until the dance begins, and I must eat supper and dress, and
    It is 5 blocks to my girl's house, and 15 additional blocks to school.
  My girl's dress will probably be ruined if we walk, because
    The sidewalks will probably be wet, because
      It has been raining this week
    And she is wearing a formal dress, which will probably touch the ground.
  I will feel like a "piker" if I make her walk, because
    Jim Brown and Ron Fuller are taking their girls to the dance in cars.

We see that evidence and conclusion are connected by a reasoning process called inference; and that argument consists of presenting conclusions and the evidence which tends to support them. But what enables us to make inferences? Why do we infer that the sidewalks will probably be wet from the fact that the week has been rainy? How do you know you can't eat supper, dress, and walk 20 blocks in an hour? The answer is simple: you know these things from past experience. You remember other rainy periods and you have found on other occasions how much (or little) can be accomplished in an hour. "But," you protest, "when I made these inferences in my mind, I didn't take time to review all my past experience with rain. The inference just came to me."

That is almost true. Long ago you observed wet sidewalks during rain X; later during rain Y; still later during rain Z. You then generalized that any rain means wet sidewalks. This process is called *induction;* from seeing particular instances you reached a generalization. This and thousands of other general statements become part of our mental equipment.

Once we have a general statement, we can easily apply it in a specific case. When rain comes along, we know this means wet sidewalks. This application to a particular case is called *deduction*. We know the general statement: any rainy day means wet sidewalks. Since this week we are having rain, we know this means wet sidewalks.

This rather extended illustration may make clear the relationships of evidence, inference, reasoning, argument, induction and deduction. Let's now examine these concepts on a more formal basis as they operate in more complex problems.

EVIDENCE AND INFERENCE[1]

Evidence consists of facts which *tend* to support a conclusion or assertion. Facts are circumstances or events which almost everyone agrees have occurred, exist, or are "true." Any reasonable person should be able to investigate a fact and find approximately what was reported by others.

Suppose cattlemen in a drouth-stricken area assert that the government should give them emergency financial assistance. The evidence they offer to support this assertion is that 200,000 acres of pasture are dried up, one million

---

[1] No attempt will be made in this chapter to cover in any complete manner the intricacies of evidence, inference, reasoning, induction, deduction, and fallacies. The reader should consult books on argumentation and logic for further elaboration of these matters. This handbook attempts rather to present the essential concepts the discusser and debater must understand before he can participate intelligently in these activities.

head of cattle are without food, and 125,000 acres of winter hay are ruined. Any reasonable person should be able, given time, to verify this data by counting acres and cattle. This statement does not mean, of course, that there can be no dispute over "facts." Two reasonable people may dispute whether a pasture is "dried up" or hay is "ruined," because a value judgment is involved. In general, however, facts are not as subject to violent dispute as are assertions.

Look again at the assertion made by the cattlemen. From these conditions, they drew the inference that the situation was serious enough to require governmental financial assistance, and asserted the government should provide it. This inference is certainly subject to disagreement. To repeat, evidence consists of facts which only *tend* to support a conclusion or assertion; other persons may reach opposite conclusions.

Types of evidence

Evidence may be *direct;* i.e., the facts exist and relate specifically (directly) to the problem. In the case of the cattlemen, the existence of dried up pastures, ruined hay, and hungry cattle is direct evidence of serious drouth conditions. Keep in mind, however, that they are not direct evidence that the government should give financial aid. This inference is debatable; the facts only *tend* to support the conclusion in the minds of some people.

Evidence may also be *indirect;* i.e., facts exist which have an implied relation to the case. Cattlemen in this area may have borrowed $2,000,000 from banks, while in a similar period in previous years loans amounted only to $250,000, thus indirectly suggesting the seriousness of drouth conditions on the financial plight of cattlemen.

A special type of indirect evidence is *negative evidence,* which is the absence of facts. Perhaps in this area at this time of year we would expect to find cattlemen buying new cars and paying off mortgages. If we check with car dealers and banks and find the cattlemen are *not* buying cars and making mortgage payments in customary quantities, the absence of these positive indications of prosperity indirectly suggest financial difficulties of the cattlemen.

Sources of evidence

Unfortunately, there is usually neither time nor opportunity for the discusser or debater to travel to this drouth area and investigate conditions for himself. To deliberate about this problem, he must depend on evidence collected by other investigators and recorded in books, magazines, and newspapers. The report of a specialist may be called *expert testimony,* that of an observer not an expert, *ordinary testimony.* A secondhand report given by a person who did not witness conditions for himself is called *hearsay,* and carries little weight.

REASONING AND ARGUMENT

Perhaps you have noted what a long, uncertain "mental leap" is involved in moving from the fact of dried up pastures to the conclusion that the government should give financial aid. Not one inference is involved here, but many. How does the discusser and debater proceed from the evidence he has gathered to a rational proposal at the policy level?

First, he examines the conclusions which the facts tend to support in his own mind. This process of studying facts and making inferences is *reasoning.* The discusser usually confines himself to reasoning aloud with other participants. The debater goes one step further. He has reached conclusions which to him seem justifiable. He then presents them in the form of *argument,* and urges his audience to agree that the facts tend to establish the results he has presented. He uses *reasoning* to demonstrate the acceptability and soundness of his conclusions.

Discussers and debaters must be satisfied that the inferences they are drawing are sound ones. How do we decide when inferences are sound? What we must have is a system of *organizing* a complex set of facts and inferences into a form which will enable us to test the soundness of our reasoning. We have such a system, based on past experience. It has two closely related parts: *induction* and *deduction.* We have learned that we may examine the facts of many situations and if we find similarities we may reach a general conclusion which will apply to all the situations. One form in which reasoning may be structured involves moving from particular cases to general conclusions; this form is induction. In the other form, deduction, we apply the generalization in a particular case. To test our inferences, we check to see if they conform to these established structural patterns of sound reasoning.

INDUCTION

As we have seen, we learn inductively. A child may be burned by a match; later he may burn himself on a radiator, a stove, or an electric iron. Perhaps he does not get burned himself but sees someone else receive a burn from these objects. He reaches a generalization: all hot things burn. Of course, some adult may supply him with this general statement before he arrives at it for himself, but the adult has learned it from experience, and the child will realize it on his own if given time.

Four kinds of induction are (a) specific instances; (b) analogy; (c) causal relationship; and (d) authority.

a. *Specific instances.* This first type is the simplest. From an examination of a sufficient number of particular cases, we draw a generalization. Cattlemen A, B, C . . . N have pastures which are dried up. Generalization: all cattlemen in this area have pastures which are dried up.[2]

Notice how natural it is to make a *deduction* now. Does Cattleman D, who is a neighbor of Cattleman C, have pastures which are dried up? Probably he does, since all cattlemen in this area do.

b. *Analogy.* In deciding what to do in a particular situation, we may find guidance from similar cases. Should the government give financial aid to drouth-stricken cattlemen? What has the government done for other citizens in like circumstances? In using analogy, we examine what action was desirable in similar (analogous) situations, and reason that the same policy would be desirable in the case under consideration. If the government found it wise to help farmers during drouth or flood conditions at other times, then perhaps aid for these cattlemen is reasonable.

The soundness of analogy depends on the resemblance of the cases. If the situations being compared are not alike in some essential respect, the conclusion drawn will not be sound. The example given here is a *literal analogy*. We compare cattlemen and farmers; both groups are citizens earning a living on the land. The groups are literally alike. Another kind of comparison, *figurative analogy,* is based

---

[2] It is wise to insert the word "probably" as you think about any generalization.

on the resemblance of objects of different classes. We speak of nations as neighbors, who build fences (tariff barriers) and keep ferocious dogs (armies) for protection. Figurative comparison often violates the principle of essential resemblance. Its greatest value is in making complex situations clear; it should be used cautiously as argument.

c. *Causal relation*. In this form of induction, we attempt to trace causes and effects. We assume that a condition does not spring into existence without a cause. We also have observed that causes produce expected effects. If the invasion of another nation's territory (cause) resulted in war (effect) in case A, B, C . . . N, we reason that invasion of any nation's territory will (probably) lead to war.

One kind of causal relationship is *cause to effect*. We assert that governmental financial aid for drouth-stricken cattlemen (cause) will bring certain desirable results (effects). How do we justify the inference? We base it on examination of other cases in which these causes brought about these effects.

Another kind is *effect to cause*. Here we recognize a condition which exists (effect) and attempt to explain what caused it. We reason that the cattlemen's serious financial plight (effect) is caused by drouth. In order to establish this relationship, we must show the absence of other causes which could have produced the same effect, such as mismanagement or poor planning of crops.

Effect to effect is a third type of causation where we reason from one effect to another effect resulting from the same cause. Increased prosperity of cattlemen will be the effect of governmental financial aid; we can then say that an additional effect will be increased prosperity for the whole nation.

d. *Authority*. This type of inference is one in which

those persons presumably in a position to "know" are cited as favoring a course of action. The speaker asserts that his proposal is sound because authorities A, B, C . . . N recommend it. The deliberator must recognize the limitations of argument from authority. All "experts" will not often agree that a single proposal is wisest. Moreover, citing authorities does not *prove* the point. It merely suggests that persons other than the speaker, presumably more qualified than the speaker, think this course is wise. In this sense, such citations help the speaker's case. He should not rely on one or two authorities, nor should he depend solely on this type of support.

DEDUCTION

We said that the child learns "hot things burn" by induction. His future behavior in a given situation, however, will be based on a deductive application of the general rule. When he sees a hot stove, even one he has never seen before, he knows not to touch it because it will burn. Deduction, which is reasoning from a general statement (called a major premise) to a particular case, can be arranged in a logical pattern called a *syllogism:*

All hot things burn. (Major premise established inductively)
This stove is a hot thing. (Minor premise: particular case)
This stove will burn. (Conclusion)

This form is a *categorical* syllogism.[3] The major premise asserts that *every* member of the class or category (all hot

---

[3] The example given is only one of many kinds of categorical syllogisms. Other variations depend on what in logic is called the figure (where the middle term appears in the syllogism) and the mood (the way in which the three statements are worded and combine into a pattern). Here we have presented the simplest and most familiar form.

things) has the characteristic indicated (burn). The minor premise says that a particular object (stove) is a member of the general category (hot things). The conclusion then follows: the particular object has the characteristic of all members of the general class.

This syllogism has three *terms* as well as three statements (two premises and a conclusion). It is important to be capable of identifying the terms in order to test the validity of the syllogism, as we shall see later. The two parts of the conclusion are called the *minor* term (stove) and the *major* term (burns). Notice that the minor term also appears in the minor premise, and the major term also appears in the major premise. The third term is called the *middle* term. In this example, the middle term is "all hot things" and it also appears twice.

There are two other commonly recognized syllogistic forms. The name *hypothetical syllogism* is usually applied to a form in which the major premise expresses a condition (if this happens . . .). The minor premise may affirm the conditional statement (called the *antecedent*):

> If nation A becomes an aggressor, nation B will retaliate.
> Nation A will become an aggressor.
> Therefore, nation B will retaliate.

The minor premise may also deny the *consequent* (the second part of the major premise):

> If nation A becomes an aggressor, nation B will retaliate.
> Nation B will not retaliate.
> Therefore, nation A will not become an aggressor.

An *alternative syllogism,* as the name implies, offers two possibilities in the major premise. The minor premise denies one alternative, and we are forced to accept the other:

> Either production will be maintained at present levels, or unemployment will increase.
> Production will not be maintained at present levels.
> Therefore, unemployment will increase.

Or:

> Either production will be maintained at present levels, or unemployment will increase.
> Unemployment will not increase.
> Therefore, production will be maintained at present levels.

Unhappily, the discusser and debater will find few such neat syllogisms as these while he is deliberating on political, economic, and social problems. There is a human factor in such matters. All hot things burn, but a given nation will not always react in the same manner even when conditions look similar. There are too many variables. The best we can hope to do is establish the *probability* of a given outcome. We may have shown inductively through causal reasoning that invasion of any nation's territory will probably lead to war. When constructing a syllogism we are wise to insert the word "probably," thus:

> Invasion of any nation's territory will *probably* lead to war.
> Nation A has invaded nation B's territory.
> Therefore, nation A's invasion will *probably* lead to war.

It must also be pointed out that the syllogism with its two premises and conclusion is rarely spelled out completely in speeches. One part is usually implied but not stated: "The United States should oppose Russian control over the nations of western Europe, since this would be to the military disadvantage of the United States." This argument can be put into syllogistic form by supplying the implied major premise:

> Any action which is to the military disadvantage of the United States should be opposed by the United States.
> Russian control over the nations of western Europe would be to the military disadvantage of the United States.
> Russian control over the nations of western Europe should be opposed by the United States.

When a premise or conclusion is implied but not stated, the form is called an *enthymeme.*

The deliberator needs to understand induction and deduction in order to be able to test the soundness of his own reasoning and that of others. These forms can be extremely complex and it is easy to become confused. We must turn now to an examination of the ways in which thinking can go wrong.

FALLACIOUS REASONING

All thinking is subject to error, and the discusser and debater must be cautious in using induction and deduction. Errors in reasoning may be detected by applying the tests suggested by the questions in the following sections.

Evidence and inference

Are the facts "true"?

Have the facts been reported accurately?

Was the observer who reported the facts competent, unprejudiced, honest?

Are the facts relevant to the conclusions they allegedly support?

Does the conclusion follow from the facts? A conclusion based on materials which are unrelated creates what is called a *non sequitur* (it does not follow).

Specific instances

Have a sufficient number of instances been examined to justify a generalization about the whole class? *Hasty generalization* results if we observe one student cheating on an examination and conclude that the whole student body is dishonest.

Are the instances examined representative or typical of the whole group? Study of a *biased* sample will lead to a fallacious generalization. We cannot draw conclusions about world health from conditions in India, Nigeria, and Arabia.

Are there negative instances or exceptions? Defenders of the present system of electing the President say it has been responsive to the will of the people, but the election of 1888 put Harrison in the White House even though Cleveland had more popular votes. This negative instance casts doubt on the generalization.

Analogy

Are the two cases being compared alike in all essential respects, or are there important points of difference? In testing the assertion that the United States would benefit from national health insurance in the same way that Britain has benefited, we would ask whether medical, social, and economic conditions in the United States are similar to those in Britain.

Causal relation

Is there actually a causal relation between the two phenomena, or is the reasoning based on *false cause?* One circumstance (breaking a mirror) may precede another circumstance (bad luck) without being responsible for it. This fallacy is called *post hoc, ergo propter hoc* (after this, therefore because of this). Also, that which is not the cause may be taken for the cause *(non causa pro causa)*. Two mountaineers taking their first train ride bought two bananas, a fruit they had never seen. Just as Jeb bit into his, the train entered a tunnel. "Have you et your banana yet?" asked Jeb. "Nope." "Well, don't. I just bit mine and I've gone blind."

Was this cause sufficient to produce the alleged effect? The conclusion that the United Nations will be successful with the United States as a member since the League of Nations failed because the United States failed to join must be carefully scrutinized. There were many complex causes for the failure of the League and the absence of the United States was only one of them.

Authority

Is the authority competent in the matters on which he is being quoted? A physicist is competent to explain how an atom bomb explodes, but his opinion on the wisdom of using the bomb in war is no better than that of any other citizen.

Has the authority been in a position to observe? A doctor is qualified to evaluate medical care but he may not be an acceptable authority on Britain's national health insurance program unless he has observed the program firsthand or made a careful study from reliable reports of persons who have observed it firsthand.

Is the authority prejudiced? An audience would not be surprised if a general in the army favored a large standing army. If a speaker wants to support a large army, he should use as authorities persons who have no bias for that position and have nothing to gain from such a policy. In fact, authorities who may lose by the policy and yet who favor a large army (often called *reluctant witnesses*) would be ideal for this speaker's purpose.

Does the authority have a reputation for honesty and accuracy?

Categorical syllogisms

Is the middle term distributed; i.e., does the middle term (all hot things, in our example) include *every* member of this whole class of objects? If the middle term covers only *some* of the members of the class of objects, we could not be certain of the conclusion:

Some students complete their assignments on time.
John is a student.
John completes his assignments on time.

This syllogism is invalid. If there are two kinds of students —those who complete their assignments on time and those who do not—we cannot be sure to which group John belongs.

Is the major premise "true"? A syllogism is logically valid if it follows certain prescribed rules of form. To test its *structural* validity, we ignore what the premises are talking about. This syllogism is *structurally* valid:

All Americans are Frenchmen.
John is an American.
Therefore, John is a Frenchman.

Obviously, this is ridiculous nonsense. Nevertheless, the form of the syllogism is *structurally* adequate. *If* all Americans were Frenchmen, and if John were an American, he would be a Frenchman. It is clear, then, that in addition to testing the structural validity of a syllogism, the deliberator wants to know whether the premises are sound. Is it true that invasion of any nation's territory will lead to war? The discusser and debater must establish the credibility of this premise before drawing conclusions from it.

Is the minor premise "true"? Did nation A actually invade nation B's territory?

Hypothetical syllogism

Does the minor premise affirm the antecedent? If the minor premise affirms the consequent, the syllogism is invalid:

> *Valid* (affirms the antecedent)
>> If the school burns to the ground, classes will be dismissed.
>> The school will burn to the ground.
>> Therefore, classes will be dismissed.
> *Invalid* (affirms the consequent)
>> If the school burns to the ground, classes will be dismissed.
>> Classes will be dismissed.
>> Therefore, the school will burn to the ground.

Classes may be dismissed for any number of reasons.

Does the minor premise deny the consequent? If it denies the antecedent, the syllogism is invalid:

Valid (denies the consequent)
    If we are to produce a play, we must have actors.
    We do not have actors.
    Therefore, we cannot produce a play.
Invalid (denies the antecedent)
    If we are to produce a play, we must have actors.
    We cannot produce a play.
    Therefore, we do not have actors.

Again, there might be many reasons for our inability to produce a play.

Alternative syllogism

Does the minor premise deny one of the alternatives? If it affirms one possibility, we can draw no conclusion.

Valid (denies one alternative)
    Either taxes must be increased or the size of the armed
        forces must be reduced.
    Taxes will not be increased.
    Therefore, the size of the armed forces must be reduced.
Invalid (affirms one alternative)
    Either taxes must be increased or the size of the armed
        forces must be reduced.
    Taxes will be increased.
    Therefore, the size of the armed forces will not be reduced.

This syllogism is invalid because taxes could be increased and the armed forces might still be reduced for other reasons.

Are the only two possible courses of action given in the major premise? The major weakness in the alternative syllogism is the "either . . . or" structure. In most complex problems of the type found in deliberation, there are more than two possibilities. In the example given, there are obviously other possibilities for maintaining the armed forces constant: nonmilitary expenses could be cut; more money could be printed; the armed forces could economize or increase efficiency; etc. If there are other alternatives, the reasoning based on this major premise will be unsound.

SUBSTITUTION OF EMOTIONAL THINKING

Persons who feel their ideas will not prevail on rational grounds may be tempted to substitute emotional thinking. They hope their nonrationality will provide a smokescreen. They are like the young lawyer who said: "My case is weak so I will attack the opposing lawyer." Emotionalism is not necessarily intentional, of course. All of us may be guilty at times of using these devices without realizing it.

1. Does the argument attack the source rather than the idea? This fallacy is called *argumentum ad hominem* or "poisoning the well." It is an attack on the man rather than his idea: Senator Jones opposes foreign aid, but he cannot be followed since he beats his wife.

2. Are we asked to accept the argument *only* because others have accepted it? A policy may or may not be sound even if it has been accepted by millions of people, by respected authorities, or by many generations of our ancestors.

a. *Band wagon.* "Everybody's doing it; you should do it, too." "Everybody" may be misguided.

b. *Argumentum ad verecundiam* (appeal to authority). "This must be so; my uncle told me." "This must be a good product; all the movie stars endorse it." Before we accept argument from authority, we must apply the tests of authority already suggested earlier in this chapter. Furthermore, we want corroboration of soundness. We should not accept a policy just because "they" say it is wise.

c. *Appeal to tradition.* "This policy is wise because the founding fathers favored it." "It was good enough for grandfather, and it's good enough for me." Times may have changed, and we need not accept a policy merely because it has been long established. At least the policy needs a fresh examination in light of current conditions.

3. Is the argument based on itself? This fallacy may take the form of *arguing in a circle* or *begging the question.* Here the conclusion may be based on an argument which is merely a restatement of the conclusion: "Persons who do not go to Church will not go to Heaven, because Heaven is reserved for those who go to Church."

4. Has the reasoner *shifted ground?* Here an argument offered to support a conclusion is not related to the conclusion. He may pretend to reply but close inspection will show that his reasons don't actually concern the matter in question.

EXERCISES

1. Select from your experience a situation like the one described in this chapter where a young man was asking for the family car. Write a report in which you (a) analyze the situation by listing the relevant facts and inferences; and (b) present an outline of the arguments and evidence you used to persuade.

2. Find (a) in current newspaper and magazine advertisements; (b) in newspaper editorials; and (c) in public speeches examples of each of the following types of inductive and deductive support:

    (1) specific instances
    (2) analogy
    (3) causal relation
    (4) authority
    (5) categorical syllogism
    (6) hypothetical syllogism
    (7) alternative syllogism.

3. Write a report in which you apply the tests of argument to each of the types of support found for exercise 2.

4. Give an example of

    (1) indirect evidence
    (2) negative evidence
    (3) expert testimony
    (4) hearsay.

5

Types of Discussion

There is much confusion in the names given to different kinds of activities called "discussion." Laymen and authors alike disagree as to what is a panel or a round table. On two matters, however, there is general agreement:

1. To be called discussion, an event must be more than a casual encounter of two friends on a street-corner who stop to "discuss" the weather. A general conversational interchange at a social gathering—or a "bull-session" where the topics "discussed" shift at random from sports to politics to education to the people present and absent—is not discussion as it is used here.
2. There are two broad categories of discussions: (a) those which are "closed"; i.e., where only the persons talking are involved in the interchange of ideas; participants talk to each other and not to a listening audience; and (b) those which are public, where participants direct their remarks as much to an audience as to each other. Students in forensic programs engage more often in the former than in the latter kind of discussion.

We will attempt to clarify the kinds of events within the "closed" and public discussion categories which may properly be called discussion, as the term is used here. Remember that the *name* we choose to assign each kind does not matter; what is important is the process going on in each activity.

DISCUSSION FOR PARTICIPANTS ONLY

It should be made clear at the outset that persons other than the participants in a closed-group discussion may be present in the room. When schools send students to an intercollegiate discussion meeting, participants from various colleges assemble in small groups and discuss. A critic-judge is usually present to evaluate the performance of each participant. Other persons may attend to observe what is taking place. Nevertheless, the members of the group talk only to each other. The judge and any observers are actually "overhearing" what is being said, and they are not treated as an audience would be treated in public discussion.

Nonpublic discussions may be further subdivided according to the two purposes they may serve: (a) policy determination; and (b) self-enlightenment.

Discussion to determine policy

The student in a forensic program engages more often in discussion to decide on policy than in any other kind. Representatives from two or more high schools or colleges gather at a centrally located institution and discuss such questions as: "How can the U. S. best combat the internal threat of communism?" and "What changes, if any, should be made in the system of electing the President of the United States?" The host school usually notifies participants well in advance so they may study the problem and often sends suggested discussion outlines and reading lists.

These groups are what we called in Chapter 1 *recommendation groups,* since the outcome of their deliberation will be a recommendation to the Congress or some other body which has authority to act in such matters.

The kinds of closed-group policy-determination discussion most frequently used when schools meet together for a discussion conference are (1) problem-solving panel; (2) legislative assembly; and (3) discussion-advocacy-legislative "progression."

1. Problem-solving panel

When students arrive, they are assigned to small groups. Usually each member of a group is from a different school. The group begins with a problem stated as a discussion question and works toward consensus on a solution. During the first round, or period of an hour or more, they may attempt to define the terms of the question and analyze the problem. A second round may be devoted to agreeing on goals or standards by which any solution must be evaluated. Additional rounds may then be given over to consideration of solutions. Participants may be judged during each round on their ability to analyze, to contribute information, to work cooperatively with the group, and similar attributes.

Participation is informal, spontaneous, and conversational. Members do not give planned "speeches." A designated leader guides the discussion, asks questions to elicit thorough coverage of the problem, and summarizes the conclusions reached.

2. Legislative assembly

When schools hold a legislative assembly or student congress, participants practice the stages in deliberation used by state legislatures and the Congress. Each member is assigned to a committee, where bills proposing action are drafted; these bills are then considered in a parliamentary assembly.

a. *Committee*. Each committee is a subgroup which is charged by the parent body (all members who meet in the parliamentary assembly) with the responsibility of investigating a specific phase of the larger problem and making a recommendation for action. The committee must decide and report. There is not always time and opportunity for the group to reach consensus; matters are often decided by majority vote. The minority may present its own recommendations to the parent group if the disagreement is crucial.

The committee may have a designated chairman, or may elect one after it assembles in committee session. The chairman is allowed to be a vigorous participant as well as the leader. Indeed, he is often made chairman because of his special knowledge of, or strong feelings on, the committee's business. He cannot be expected to be an impartial leader, even though this may be the ideal in other kinds of discussion.

The work of each committee varies with its specific assignment. When the Illinois Legislative Assembly discussed a federal program of wage and price control, four committees considered substantive matters: committee on wage stabilization, committee on price stabilization, committee on federal budget and taxation, and committee on monetary policy. In addition, four committees handled procedural matters: credentials, rules, nominations, and resolutions.

b. *Parliamentary assembly*. Climax of the student congress occurs when the whole group meets as a unicameral or bicameral assembly. Here bills are reported out of committees, debated, and voted on. The parliamentary assembly operates under formal rules of procedure. Members may speak only after being recognized by the chairman and debate must relate to the motion before the house.

Occasionally an assembly may employ a less formal kind of discussion by considering a particular proposal in a *committee of the whole*. The motion which brings about this change is: "I move that the assembly resolve itself into a committee of the whole for the purpose of considering this matter." What follows is informal interchange of ideas without formal rules for controlling debate.

Joint committee sessions, party caucuses, and joint conferences of representatives from the two houses are other variations of discussion which may be utilized during a legislative assembly.

c. *Discussion-advocacy-legislative "progression."* Similar to the student congress is this type of activity which also proceeds from small-group discussion to legislative consideration of proposed bills. Instead of following Congressional committee format and having substantive and procedural committees, its first stages are much like the deliberation of the problem-solving panels already mentioned. Members are assigned to small groups and each group defines, analyzes, considers goals, and weighs possible solutions. After attitudes are crystallized as a result of discussion, participants in the next stage deliver speeches advocating their particular solution(s) to the problem. The final stage is a legislative assembly which debates and votes on specific proposals.

Discussion for self-enlightenment

Closed-group discussion may serve a second general purpose: that of enlightening the members of a group. Students in many forensic programs use this kind of discus-sion in preparing for participation in interschool debate. When a national topic for debate is announced, they begin their study by conducting discussions on various phases of the problem. They may hold a series of meetings on such questions as: How should the terms in the proposition be defined? What are the immediate causes for considering this problem? What are the historical origins of this con-troversy? What is the nature of the problem? What are the main issues in this controversy?

Here emphasis is on investigating and learning. Whether or not what goes on is discussion depends on how the meet-ing is conducted. If group effort is directed toward finding out about a definite phase of the problem, questions are raised, members all contribute information relevant to the questions, and the outcome is a summary of the ideas con-tributed by the whole group, then the discussion method is being followed. The spirit of discussion is violated if the leader attempts to reach a predetermined outcome, encour-ages answers which further it, rejects information which leads away from it, and supplies the desired outcome if the group does not reach it. There is nothing "wrong" or "bad" about this latter method of conducting a meeting; much of education is carried on in this manner. It just is not dis-cussion as we are defining that term.

PUBLIC DISCUSSION

The purposes of public discussion may also be to en-lighten those listening or to determine policy. Any of the types mentioned here could be utilized for either purpose.

Students may participate in *panel* discussion before an audience. Members contribute as they do in the closed-group panel already described; the most important change introduced by the presence of the audience is that participants engage in interchange of ideas for the benefit of the listeners. This kind of discussion is often used for programs presented to civic clubs and women's groups. The panel format is also employed extensively when student discussion is broadcast by radio or television.

Another variation of public discussion is the *symposium*. In this type, two or more speakers present their ideas on the problem. They deliver planned speeches without interruption. Speakers usually represent different points of view. In a symposium on a policy of free trade, for example, the four speakers could deal with free trade as it would affect the domestic producer, the domestic consumer, nations friendly to the United States, and nations unfriendly to the United States.

In the situations described thus far, the listening audience is passive. It is customary at the conclusion of such discussions to invite the audience to question the participants and make comments. To distinguish between the two parts of the program, it is convenient to label this audience participation period a *forum*. (Actually the whole meeting can properly be called a forum; the word harks back to the Roman public square where public business was conducted.) Thus, we can have a panel-forum, when the formal discussion is followed by listener participation. Symposia are almost always set up in symposium-forum arrangement. Another variation is the symposium-panel-forum, where the speakers give their set speeches, then sit down and discuss as a panel, and finally invite audience reaction.

EXERCISES

1. Write a report in which you describe what happened in a committee meeting you have attended. Decide whether the committee session should be called discussion, as we are using the term, and suggest any ways in which you feel the committee could have fulfilled its function more effectively.
2. Listen to a discussion broadcast by radio or television. Describe the method followed, and identify the type of discussion being used.
3. Study the group meetings utilized by the student council or senate in your school; classify the meetings as to types of discussion. Comment on any kinds of discussion not being used which might profitably be added.

6

Preparing for Discussion

ANALYSIS

The first step in preparing for participation in discussion is to analyze the problem. Analysis is a "taking apart," a separation of the whole into its constituent parts in order to see interrelationships. To examine a watch, a jeweler does not sit and stare at the whole timepiece from the outside; instead, he literally "takes apart" the problem by removing the case and disassembling the working parts. Only when we have broken the problem down and examined each of the components can we begin to understand the difficulties involved.

The success of analysis will depend on asking the right questions:

1. Why is this problem important now?
2. What is the nature of the problem?
3. Who is involved in the problem?
4. How can the problem be defined?
5. What is the historical background of the problem?
6. What caused the problem?
7. Is there strong disagreement as to how the problem should be solved?

Analysis will not end, of course, with this preliminary questioning and searching. Throughout discussion you will need to reanalyze in light of new material.

RESEARCH

After you have asked such questions as these about the problem, you will be anxious to find more complete answers than you have. The next stage in preparation is to do research (see Chapter 3: Finding the Facts). The discusser must be just as adequately informed as the debater. Discussion is *not* a pooling of ignorance, where participants gather casually and idly exchange opinions and notions. The individual members of a group must have facts if the sharing process is to be profitable.

Collect information from every source available to you. Keep an ever-expanding bibliography of materials. Make careful notes of everything you hear, observe, and read on the problem. Exchange ideas with friends. Only a well-informed participant makes a worth-while contribution to any discussion.

SYNTHESIS

After analyzing the problem and finding answers to the questions you have asked, you are ready to synthesize your understanding. Synthesis is the opposite of analysis. It is putting together again into an ordered whole your concept of the problem.

Perhaps the clearest form in which to record your synthesis is to write a *complete-sentence outline* containing the same divisions as the analysis, and reporting your answers to the questions. For example, one unit of the outline would begin: "This problem is important now because . . ."; this statement would be followed by subordinate presentation of the recent events which have made the problem a vital one.

This outline, prepared by the individual participant, serves much the same function for the discusser that a brief serves for the debater (see Chapter 11). It contains all the information and evidence the participant has collected on the subject. He has it before him during the discussion and refers to it for facts. Of course, the discusser may also have evidence recorded on note cards of a convenient size (see Chapter 3) and these, too, are before him while he participates.

The outline should have numerical headings to identify each statement (I, A, 1, a, B . . .). Sources of information (references to books, magazines, pamphlets) should be indicated in the left-hand margin, in footnote form at the bottom of each page, or between the lines of the outline itself.

THE GROUP OUTLINE

A problem-solving group will make better progress if it follows a systematic pattern, or group outline, which suggests the kinds of questions to be asked. The outline will usually be prepared in advance of the discussion. The leader, if one has been named, ordinarily has a hand in the preparation of the outline although other participants may help. Certainly every member must understand the pattern to be followed and should be capable of drawing up one.

The group outline serves as a guide which the leader may follow to keep the discussion "on the track." It should not serve as a strait jacket to be followed item by item without deviation. The group should be allowed to exchange ideas spontaneously and new ideas, which were not anticipated in the outline, should be forthcoming. At the same time, the group should follow in a general way the over-all pattern it sets out to pursue. It becomes the leader's responsibility to allow fruitful deviations while directing the group in the right general direction.

The pattern customarily followed in problem-solving discussion is an adaptation of John Dewey's well-known steps in reflective thinking. It begins with awareness of a problem ("felt difficulty"); the problem is defined and analyzed; possible ways of meeting the problem are considered and evaluated; the best solution is chosen and tested, if possible.

A generalized pattern for discussion follows. For a given occasion, these questions would be made specific for that particular problem. Notice that the kinds of questions which were discussed at the beginning of this chapter as a part of analysis of the problem appear in this outline in the definition and analysis stages.

Definition   I. What do the terms of the question mean?

Analysis   II. What is the nature of the problem?

      A. What are the facts of the present situation?

        1. How can the present situation best be described?

          a. *What* is going on?

          b. *Who* is involved?

          c. *What kinds* of difficulties exist?

          d. *When* did the problem develop?

          e. *Where* is the problem most serious?

          f. Have we presented enough factual

information to make the nature of
the problem clear?

    2. How serious is the problem?

       a. Is the problem extensive?

       b. Is a change urgent?

       c. Why is the problem important
now?

B. What are the causes of the problem?

    1. What is the history of the problem?

    2. What conditions brought it about?

C. What forces are at work to change the
present situation?

    1. What solutions have been tried?

       a. How extensive have these attempts
been?

       b. How successful have these attempts
been?

    2. Is there need for additional attempts
to solve the problem?

    3. What will be the probable results if
no action is taken?

D. To what extent does this group agree on
a course of action?

    1. On what matters are members agreed?

    2. On what matters are members dis-
agreed?

    3. What are the controversies which
must be worked out?

Goals   III. What standards, criteria, or goals must any
solution to the problem meet?

A. What kind of world do we want to live
in?

B. What ideals must a solution satisfy?

Possible   IV. What courses of action are possible?

Solutions	A. What is one possible solution?
	1. What is good about this possibility?
	2. What is bad about this possibility?
	B. What is another possible solution? etc.
Choosing Best Solution	V. What solution should this group choose?
Application	VI. What steps should be followed in putting this solution into effect?

Not every question suggested here will appear in the group outline for every problem. There also will be questions appropriate to a particular matter which do not appear in this generalized pattern. Nevertheless, the major steps of definition, analysis, goals, and solutions will almost always be followed.

PHYSICAL ARRANGEMENTS FOR DISCUSSION

Whenever members of a discussion group can control the environment in which they assemble, they should give some thought to physical arrangements.

1. Participants should be seated so that every person can face everyone else, if possible. If members can sit around a single table, or if chairs can be placed in a circle or semi-circle, each participant will feel that he is a part of the group.

2. Participation will be easier in most situations if the members can be seated at a table. Well-informed contributors will have notes, outlines, and reference books, and these materials are easier to manage at a table. The leader and some of the participants may want to take notes while the discussion is in progress.

3. Participants should be comfortable but not too comfortable.

4. An atmosphere of industrious informality should be encouraged. The impression to be established is that the group has met to accomplish something. At the same time, members should foster a cordial informality. The leader or some other person should arrive in the room early and greet each member. Each person can then be introduced to the others. If the members are not well acquainted, they may want to print name plates and put them in front of each individual so that everyone's name becomes familiar. Informality can be promoted by calling one another by first names.

EXERCISES

1. Prepare a *complete-sentence outline* for your individual use as a participant in a discussion on a current political or social problem; prepare a *group outline* on the same question.
2. Observe a discussion group in action; report on the physical arrangements made for the discussion.

7

Participating in Discussion

Since discussion is the cooperative effort of a group to reach a solution acceptable to all, each participant must understand the nature of his role. Discussion is characterized by reflective thinking, careful inquiry, and patient consideration of the views of others.

The participant must first of all be well informed and well prepared for his task (see Chapter 6). He must also (1) have discussion attitude; (2) exercise care in the use of language; (3) appreciate the problems of interpersonal relations; (4) develop the desirable qualities of the superior group member; and (5) avoid the undesirable traits which disrupt discussion.

DISCUSSION ATTITUDE

An absolute essential of participation is "discussion attitude." The discusser must strive to be objective, rational, impartial, and open-minded. He is searching for an answer to the question; he is not engaging in argument. He must consider the common good. He must be willing to listen carefully to others, and to modify his own ideas in the light of new evidence presented by members of the group.

The discusser should analyze his own prejudices. What factors cause him to become emotional about some suggested possibilities for action? He must try to consider the problem apart from his own emotions and feelings.

Some idea of the desired attitude can be gained from studying the "scientific attitude." The research engineer may be asked by his company to discover what weight and quality of motor oil is best and most economical for operating certain machinery. He collects a sample of every oil available, puts each one through identical tests for durability, efficiency, and economy, and decides which is best and least expensive on the basis of the measurements obtained. He does not favor one over another; he is impartial. If you can imagine a researcher who owned stock in the oil company which sells test oil No. 6, and who would report that oil No. 6 was best even though the tests did not demonstrate its superiority, then you are picturing a scientist without "scientific attitude." He has lost his objectivity.

The discusser must strive to examine a policy rationally, seeing its strengths and weaknesses apart from his personal preferences, political affiliations, or socio-economic background. A solution must rest on its merits, not on the emotional acceptability of those persons or forces supporting it.

Obstacles to objectivity

It is not always easy to be objective, rational, and open-minded. We aren't always aware of our prejudices and our emotional blocks to straight thinking. Perhaps it will be helpful to suggest in a general way some of the obstacles to objectivity.

1. Objectivity seems to vary inversely with our personal

involvement in the question for discussion. The closer the problem is to our lives, interests, and needs, the more difficult it is for us to be objective. The participant must watch himself more closely, then, when discussing such problems.

2. Objectivity seems to vary according to our past experiences and attitudes. Some people have learned to examine problems more rationally than others. Although it is foolish to try to fit people into neat pigeonholes, there seem to be "doubters," and "dogmatists," and people who say: "You'll have to *show* me." The discusser must analyze his own background carefully to see if he is harboring attitudes which are not conducive to calm investigation.

3. Our prior associations with other members of the group seem to influence our objectivity. Apparently we can be more objective in working with some people than with others. We must be aware of any personal reactions to others which influence our rationality.

CARE IN THE USE OF LANGUAGE

Fruitful discussion requires careful use of language. The consequences of the misuse of language may be misunderstanding, endless wrangling, and emotional reaction which heightens disagreement.

To say exactly what you mean in words is difficult. The complex social, economic, and political problems of deliberation intensify the difficulty. The engineer sometimes can be precise: "Lubricating oil No. 9 lubricated motor X for 285 hours and 13 minutes." The deliberator, on the other hand, cannot say: "The institution of a federal union of Atlantic Pact nations will cause an 18% improvement in East-West relations." Nevertheless, he must try to express exact meanings. Here are some suggestions:

1. Use language which is as precise and accurate as possible.

a. *Avoid ambiguity.* Be especially careful with words such as "socialism," "communism," "Americanism," and other words where the object to which the word refers is vague. Be careful also with words which have more than one meaning: "Democrat–democrat," etc.

b. *Avoid all-inclusive language.* Be careful with sweeping generalizations: "All businessmen are crooks"; "everyone likes (hates) America"; "students are lazy."

c. *Define* clearly, carefully, fully, and often. Regard a definition as a process rather than a finished product. For example, when you use the word "democracy," stop and add: "I'm referring to democracy as the form of government practiced in the United States at this moment." (The Russians say *their* system is a "people's democracy," too.) Then you might define it by describing in detail how our government works today (voting rights, trial by jury, protection from search and seizure, etc.). At the abstract *word* level, both America and Russia say they have democracies. When you start itemizing *details,* you can quickly distinguish one from the other.

2. Use language which is as objective and unemotional as possible. Be careful not to color your statements, even unintentionally, by unfortunate word choices. Try to report events without bias. An extreme example is:

Objective: Senator Jones spoke for ninety minutes in favor of federal aid to education and compulsory national health insurance.

Emotional: Senator Jones shot off his mouth in a long-winded harangue which was socialistic-communistic propaganda.

3. Be aware of the difference between denotation and connotation. Denotation is the literal meaning of a word, while connotation is the associative images the word creates in the minds of listeners. These associations depend on the background and experiences of the recipient. In a discussion on abolishing fraternities, one participant mentioned "regulated study hours." To a fraternity man in the group, this term suggested quiet study environment, an opportunity for making better grades, and other desirable associations; to a nonfraternity member in the group, the words meant regimentation, force, and unpleasant restrictions. Until they stopped to define carefully what "regulated study hours" implied, they were actually talking about two different things.

Connotation of words can be illustrated by considering the following contrasting terms.

Neutral word	Approving	Derogatory
young	childlike	childish
old (man)	mature	ancient, decrepit
attorney	counselor	ambulance-chaser
slender	sylphlike	skinny
horse	thoroughbred	nag

4. Use concrete expressions, illustrations, specific facts, and examples wherever this is possible, rather than abstractions. In discussing free trade, for example, talk about "$115,000,000 worth of electrical machinery and trucks, and 3,400 tons of steel," rather than "lots of goods and all kinds of equipment." Instead of reporting vaguely that a Senator is a "liberal," name some of the bills he has supported.

5. Avoid using words or expressions which will cause others in the group to resent your contributions.

Say	Don't Say
"Here is one idea; would you consider this . . ."	"I have the answer here; now get this . . ."
"Have you thought of this possibility?"	"Anyone who has done any reading has heard . . ."
"This makes sense to me; what do the rest of you think?"	"Let me get you straightened out; here is what we must do."

INTERPERSONAL RELATIONS

Members of discussion groups must be aware of the various ways in which other participants may be reacting to them as individuals. If you expect others to cooperate with you in working toward a desirable outcome, you must exhibit behavior which does not cause resentment.

Group cooperation is hindered if unfavorable emotional reaction toward one or two individuals is experienced. Even if participants respect a member for his knowledge and abilities, they may not like his behavior. Let's illustrate what can happen. The writer observed a discussion group where one individual, call him X, was violating these suggestions. When the leader asked a question, X was the first to answer, *every time.* Suppose member Y commented next. If Y disagreed with X, Mr. X would offer a refutation. If Y agreed with X, Mr. X would quickly add further elaboration. So it went: chairman to X; X to Y; Y to X; chairman to X; X to Z; Z to X. Reactions of the other participants could be surmised from the glances directed at X. The chairman, particularly, began to look at him with annoyance.

Another clue to the malfunctioning of the group was the extreme care everyone was exercising to be tactful toward everyone except X. Mr. X was also physically uncooperative. He had not pulled his chair up to the table, as had the others. Rather he sat sideways, and somewhat withdrawn, as if an "expert" only partially a member of the group. When not speaking, X looked down at his hands, was inattentive, and seemed bored.

In the middle of one of X's many pronouncements, a new member walked into the room. Suddenly X stopped and said: "I know this isn't my job here, but I would like to interrupt the discussion to ask this new person who *he* is." (The inflection given the word "he" seemed to ask: What business do you have walking in in the middle of my speech?") The chairman, struggling to retain her self-control, nodded weakly, and said: "Oh, yes, I was about to ask him." She couldn't have done it sooner without interrupting X!

This case of Mr. X is obviously an extreme example but it suggests the kinds of difficulties the wise participant will try to avoid.

OTHER DESIRABLE QUALITIES

There are other qualities which are important to the superior participant.

1. *Ability to speak.* You will make an outstanding contribution to the group only if you have the ability to express your ideas clearly. You should speak to be heard and understood. You should talk as you do in conversation, but this does not mean that you should not speak well and correctly. Show physical alertness. You must work at discussion; you cannot think while you are too relaxed and comfortable.

2. *Ability to listen.* Listen carefully to what others are contributing. Otherwise, you will not be able to help push

the discussion forward by building on what has been said.

3. *Enthusiasm.* Show that you *want* to consider the problem. Discussion should be a lively interchange of stimulating ideas. If you seem uninterested, you will give the impression that you are agreeing just to follow the line of least resistance. You will not seem eager to work out with others a satisfactory plan of action on a vital problem.

4. *Tact.* When you want to disagree, do so; but do it politely without injuring feelings. You can discuss ideas without condemning the persons holding those ideas. Say: "I see what you are getting at; here's the thing I thought of in that connection." Don't say: "You must be mistaken there; let me show you . . ." Be courteous. Don't speak when someone else is speaking. Be as considerate of others in the group as you would be of guests in your living room.

UNDESIRABLE QUALITIES

Below are some attributes you will be wise to avoid in discussion.

1. *Don't be dogmatic.* Don't be certain that you are right and refuse to budge, as a habitual pattern of response.

2. *Don't be an advocate.* You have a right to your convictions. You should express them confidently and the group should listen to your ideas. But don't keep coming back to a pet panacea.

3. *Don't monopolize the conversation.* The person who talks too much will encounter resentment. Do your share of contributing but don't talk too often or too long.

4. *Don't be glum and mum.* Avoid if you can being noticeably silent, moody, or irritable. You will not only fail to make your fair contribution; you will also dampen the spirits of the whole group and endanger its efforts.

5. *Don't be a mere disagreer.* Avoid saying "I disagree" without having reasons and countersuggestions.

6. *Don't hurry the solution.* Don't be so anxious to get the problem settled that you will agree to anything just to end the discussion.

7. *Don't be a mere phrasemaker.* The phrasemaker usually has no real information to contribute, but tries to get by with such comments as: "I agree"; "I think so too"; and "In my opinion we should do that."

EXERCISES

1. Observe a discussion group in action. Write a report in which you describe and evaluate the "discussion attitude" of each participant.

2. Obtain reprints of discussions broadcast by radio; make a study of the language usage of participants. Report on the presence or absence of ambiguity, inclusiveness of language, use of definition, objectivity of word choices, and so on. (Note: Reprints of *Northwestern Reviewing Stand, Chicago Round Table,* and *America's Town Meeting of the Air* are available at nominal cost.)

3. Listen to a discussion broadcast by radio or television. Record examples of good and poor participation using the qualities suggested in this chapter as a checklist.

8

Leading Discussion

In most group-deliberation situations, one member will be designated leader. It is his duty to guide the group toward successful achievement. He will do so through suggesting, encouraging, restraining, and directing. He will refrain from manipulating, driving, threatening, scolding, and dictating. His control should be deft and gentle, yet firm. The group should feel pleasurably secure under his leadership. There should be no trace of resentment.

QUALITIES

We can't, of course, expect the leader to be a super-being. We can only suggest the qualities we want while recognizing that most of us cannot measure up in every respect. Actually a person who has most of these attributes will probably be a successful leader. Through practice, moreover, he can develop his abilities and increase his effectiveness.

1. *Intelligence.* The best leader in a group is not necessarily the member with the highest I.Q. Nevertheless, he must be able to think, to reason, and to see relationships. Furthermore, he must be able to think *quickly*—it is essential that he be one jump ahead of the group in seeing where the discussion is headed and where it should go next.

2. *Knowledge.* The leader should have two kinds of

knowledge. He must know thoroughly the subject matter the group is discussing. The ideal leader will also have a deep understanding, both historical and current, of social, economic, and political problems. He must also understand discussion method and the deliberative process.

3. *Social sensitivity.* If others are to follow him, the leader must understand people, and be sensitive to their reactions (see Chapter 7). He will recognize the hostile, shy, conceited, overbearing, or reticent participant and will know what to do to increase the effectiveness of that member of the group. He should be amiable and tactful. The members should *like* him.

4. *Impartiality.* Not only should the good leader in problem-solving deliberation be fair and impartial, he should also zealously maintain the discussion attitude. He must allot time for talking fairly. He must not favor one point of view or particular contributors. He should, if necessary, encourage the group to pursue the "truth" open-mindedly. An enthusiastic leader with the right attitude can challenge members to make the discussion an exciting quest for understanding.

5. *Speech skills.* Ability to speak effectively, to express ideas clearly and fluently, is obviously vital to the good leader.

6. *Other desirable qualities.* We could ask much more of the discussion leader. He should have self-control. He needs persistence and firmness. He can profit from a sense of humor by which he puts people at ease and reduces tension in emotional crises.

DUTIES

The designated leader is usually responsible for the success of the discussion from the planning stage to the conclusion. He is concerned with (a) initial planning; (b) introducing the members and getting the discussion under way; (c) guiding, regulating, and ending the discussion; and (d) serving as chairman of the forum period if there is an audience. Of course, the leader in a particular situation may not be responsible for every phase of the discussion. The planning may be completed by others and the chairman may be selected after the participants assemble. This situation often occurs in intercollegiate discussion.

Some of the duties the leader should perform at each stage are suggested below:

1. Planning

Word the question impartially (see Chapter 2).

Invite qualified participants (see Chapter 7).

Publicize the discussion.

Help draw up a group outline and distribute a copy to members (see Chapter 6).

Learn everything he can about the problem up for discussion.

Call a prediscussion planning session for all participants. At this meeting, he should distribute a bibliography of materials on the question and suggest additional sources of information. The group at this point should talk about the terms to be defined, the information needed to analyze the problem, etc., but it must be careful *not* to have the discussion itself now, since spontaneity at the real discussion would be jeopardized.

Check on the physical arrangements of the room in which the discussion will be held (see Chapter 6).

2. Introducing

Introduce the participants to the audience, if it is a public discussion.

Get the discussion under way by announcing the question, explaining in general why the discussion has come about, and giving briefly the background information which will lead into the first question he wants to ask.

3. Guiding

Keep the discussion "on the track."

Discourage irrelevant contributions.

Ask for fuller discussion of points not being adequately covered.

Make internal summaries when the group shifts attention from one phase of the outline to the next.

See that the group makes steady progress.

Clarify and restate contributions when members seem confused.

Ask for frequent, careful definitions of terms being used.

4. Regulating

Insure evenness of contribution, restrain participants who want to monopolize the conversation, and draw out the reticent contributor.

Gently insist that members maintain the discussion attitude.

Try to restore equanimity after clashes among participants.

5. Ending

Summarize what the group has decided.

6. Leading forum period in public discussion

Have persons speaking from the floor state questions clearly. If necessary, restate the question so the participants and the whole audience have heard and understood what is being asked.

Encourage the questioner to direct his question to a specific member of the discussion group.

Protect the feelings of participants by gracefully turning aside personal attacks, insults, and the like, directed at individuals. To do so is not as difficult as it sounds. If the leader feels sure the questioner is alone among audience members who would feel it important to insist on a direct answer to a personal attack, the leader might say: "That's an interesting question, and I'm sure it could take the rest of the night for Mr. Jones to give an adequate answer; perhaps you can get a better answer if you will ask him privately after the meeting is over. Could we have another question, please?"

Try to spread audience participation as widely as possible. At best, time will be limited and relatively few people can comment or raise questions. One or a few individuals should not be allowed to monopolize the question period, to make extended remarks, or to conduct a lengthy cross-examination of the participants.

SOME SPECIAL PROBLEMS

How much authority should the leader have? We have said the leader should guide, not dictate, but should he have the power to "make" a member quit talking? If two members disagree on a definition of a term, should the chairman be allowed to decide which one will be used? If the leader wants to do one thing, and the group another, who wins?

There is another special problem. Shouldn't the leader have an opportunity to contribute his own opinions, concepts, and factual information? Must he be a nonpartisan? Can't he be a participant as well as the leader and still be impartial and fair in allotting time to various factions?

There is an army expression which is the easiest answer to these questions. Officers answering questions about troop dispositions in a tactical problem often say: "that depends on the situation and the terrain." The leader's authority and participation depend on the kind of discussion and, above all, on the desires of the group.

1. In a parliamentary assembly, the presiding officer is given extensive authority. His powers are specified in a body of rules accepted through long usage (*Robert's Rules,* etc.). When a speaker's time is up, the chairman can require him to stop. Why is he given such power? There are good reasons: (a) time is usually limited; (b) the group may need to consider several complex problems in one meeting; and (c) large numbers of persons are involved. Also, the chairman appears to have more power than he has in fact. Almost all his decisions are subject to appeal and overthrow by a majority of the members. The real authority in a democratic group resides in the group itself.

In an informal problem-solving group of a few members, the leader can have whatever power the group is willing to give him. Obviously, authoritarian control is out of place here. How much control the group will want the leader to exercise will depend "on the situation and the terrain."

2. In most group discussions, the leader can function best as an impartial guide who asks questions, directs and summarizes, but who does not express his own slant on the problem or contribute information except perhaps when something important has been overlooked. By limiting himself to these functions, he contributes to the willingness

of members to deliberate cooperatively; if he becomes a partisan, members who hold opposite convictions may feel that their ideas will not get a fair hearing.

The chairman of a committee, of course, should be allowed to participate in the group's decisions. Often he is made chairman because he has more knowledge of the problem than the others.

EXERCISES

1. Listen to a discussion broadcast by radio or television. Write a report on the discussion leader in which you comment on the following questions:
    a. Did the leader guide the discussion successfully?
    b. Did the leader follow a pattern?
    c. Did the leader give adequate internal summaries?
    d. Was the leader's final summary a fair statement of the group's views?
2. Consider two discussion situations: (a) a committee charged with planning a dance for a school activity group; and (b) a discussion group composed of the head of the school (chairman), two members of the faculty, and two representatives of the student body meeting to establish school policy on student class attendance. Write a report in which you compare the functions of the discussion leaders in these two situations.
3. Compare the functions of the leader of a panel and the chairman of a symposium.
4. Write a report in which you compare the qualities you would expect in a committee chairman, a leader of a panel, and the chairman of a symposium.

9

Evaluating
Discussion

Discussions in the Congressional committee, the foreign ministers conference, and the town hall are judged by their *outcomes,* not by the techniques or procedures employed. Participants and hearers consider the discussion successful if they acquired new information, saw or experienced attitude change and were satisfied with the decisions reached. To design an evaluation sheet for these discussions, we ask questions of the following kind, and answer each question with a judgment as to whether this discussion was above average, average, or below average in each respect.

Did Participants and Audience	(Check each continuum at the point which represents your judgment)
1. Acquire new information?	(Above Av.) (Average) (Below Av.)
2. Change attitudes?	(Above Av.) (Average) (Below Av.)
3. Reach acceptable decisions?	(Above Av.) (Average) (Below Av.)

We are also concerned here with participants who are *learning* about discussion *techniques and procedures.* In addition to evaluating outcomes, we must set up criteria for judging the whole process involved in discussion. Here is a rating scale for participants:

Judge's Evaluation Report on Participants

Name of participant...

Assign the participant for each criterion one of the following ratings: 5—Superior; 4—Excellent; 3—Good; 2—Below Average; 1—Poor.

Criteria	*Rating*
1. *Attitude.* Objectivity, open-mindedness; willingness to modify views in light of new evidence.	....
2. *Knowledge.* Information on the problem.	....
3. *Thinking.* Analysis, ability to reason about the problem.	....
4. *Listening.* Ability to understand and interpret views of others.	....
5. *Speaking.* Ability to communicate ideas clearly and effectively; adaptation to the speaking situation.	....
6. *Consideration for others.* Tact, courtesy, cooperation; evenness of contribution.	....

Note that the criteria for judging the performance of the participant are similar to the characteristics of the superior group member described in Chapter 7. Questions about the meanings of these criteria can probably be cleared up by reviewing that chapter.

The group leader, when he is an impartial guide, must be judged on a different rating sheet. Again, these criteria follow the suggestions in Chapter 8 on leadership.

Judge's Evaluation Report on the Leader

Name of leader...

Assign for each criterion one of the following ratings:
5—Superior; 4—Excellent; 3—Good; 2—Below Average;
1—Poor.

Criteria	*Rating*
1. *Thinking.* Ability to think quickly, to see relationships.	....
2. *Knowledge.* Understanding of the problem. Knowledge of discussion method.	....
3. *Attitude.* Impartiality, fairness; ability to help group maintain discussion attitude.	....
4. *Speaking.* Ability to express ideas clearly, rephrase unclear contributions.	....
5. *Introducing.* Skill in getting the discussion off to a good start.	....
6. *Guiding.* Ability to keep discussion "on the track"; maintain progress; make internal summaries.	....
7. *Regulating.* Insuring evenness of contribution; maintaining equanimity.	....
8. *Ending.* Summarizing group effort.	....

EXERCISES

1. Observe a discussion group in action. Rate the leader and each participant, using the type of scales suggested here. Then write a report in which you indicate whether you feel the rating scales convey an accurate evaluation of the discussion. If you feel the scales are inadequate, suggest changes or additions.
2. Design a rating scale for evaluating the leader's performance in a committee situation where the leader is both chairman and participant.

10

Types of Debate

TRADITIONAL DEBATE

Traditional debate is the type most familiar to those who debate in school. Here two sides, affirmative and negative, are given equal amounts of time and speak in a predetermined order, with the affirmative having the opening constructive speech and the closing rebuttal speech. Each debater speaks twice, once as a constructive speaker and again in rebuttal.

There could be any number of speakers on each side, and the speeches could be of any length, but the form which has become most common today has two members on the affirmative team and two on the negative. Constructive speeches are ten minutes in length, rebuttal speeches, five. Order of speaking is:

> *Constructive speeches:*
> First affirmative
> First negative
> Second affirmative
> Second negative.
>
> *Rebuttal speeches:*
> First negative
> First affirmative
> Second negative
> Second affirmative.

The two members of each team work together to present a unified *case* in support of their side of the proposition. The case is advanced in the constructive speeches. Rebuttal speeches allow debaters to attack the case of the opposition and to defend their own.

This orthodox pattern of debate is similar to the speaking which occurs in the courtroom, where attorneys for the prosecution and the defense alternate in offering constructive argument and then rebuttal.

PARLIAMENTARY DEBATE

This form is much like the debate which goes on in a legislature, the Congress, or the British House of Commons. A chairman presides to recognize speakers, maintain order, and conduct business. The opposing sides usually sit facing each other, with chairs placed at right angles to the front of the room. It is customary for the *principal* speakers for and against the resolution to be notified in advance so that they may prepare.

When the meeting is called to order by the chairman, the resolution to be debated is introduced and seconded. The chair then recognizes the mover of the resolution, who proceeds to speak in its support. The first main speaker against the motion speaks next. He is followed by the next principal speaker for the motion, and so on.

After the appointed speakers have been heard, the chairman asks if there is further discussion. General debate continues, under rules adopted by the house, until there is sentiment to end debate and vote on the resolution. The question is decided by "division of the house"; i.e., by allowing members to vote for or against the resolution.

Procedure for this type of debate can best be illustrated

by including the special rules followed in the monthly parliamentary debates of the Illini Forensic Association at the University of Illinois:

All members of the audience are encouraged to speak from the floor, and to express convictions on the resolution before the assembly, under the following special rules:

1. The audience will seat itself according to sentiment on the resolution. Those who are for the resolution as it is stated should sit on the chairman's right (as he faces the audience). The opposition should sit on the chairman's left.

2. There will be two principal speakers for, and two against, the resolution. The first speaker for the resolution will read it, move its adoption by the assembly, and be recognized as the first speaker for the resolution. Maximum time for principal speakers is seven minutes; at the end of six minutes the chairman will rap his gavel to warn the speaker that he has one minute remaining. When the seven minutes have passed, the chair will ask the speaker to conclude his remarks.

3. Principal speakers will not be subject to interruption.

4. At the conclusion of the principal speeches, general debate will be in order. The chair will ask: "Is there further discussion?" The chairman will recognize speakers from the floor under the following rules:

    a. The method of getting the floor is to rise, and to address the chairman: "Mr. Chairman."

    b. The chairman will recognize speakers from the floor for three minutes.

    c. The chairman will recognize speakers alternately for and against the resolution.

    d. Principal speakers may speak in the general debate. However, the chairman will recognize a speaker who has not spoken previously before recognizing a member who has spoken.

e. Any speaker may interrupt a speaker from the floor by rising, and without waiting to be recognized, address the chair: "Mr. Chairman, will the speaker yield for a question (or observation, or comment)?" The chairman will ask the speaker if he is willing to be interrupted, or the speaker may at once decline or accept. If the speaker yields, the interruption will not be included in his speaking time.

5. All speakers will be confined to speaking on the resolution before the assembly.

6. Debate may be ended by general consent (if no one wishes to speak further), or by a motion to end debate. The proper form of this motion is: "Mr. Chairman, I move to end debate." To carry, this motion requires a ⅔ vote.

7. The motion to adjourn may not be offered until there has been a vote on the resolution.

8. The resolution before the house may be amended. This motion requires a majority vote. A motion to amend may be hostile but it must be related to the resolution.

9. Any question not covered by these special rules will be decided in accordance with *Robert's Rules of Order,* revised.

CROSS-EXAMINATION DEBATE

Another form of debate which has borrowed heavily from the courtroom is cross-examination debating. Developed at the University of Oregon, it involves:

1. a. First affirmative speech.
   b. Cross-examination by first negative speaker.
2. a. First negative speech.
   b. Cross-examination by second affirmative speaker.

3. a. Second affirmative speech.
   b. Cross-examination by second negative speaker.
4. a. Second negative speech.
   b. Cross-examination by first affirmative speaker.
5. Summation and rebuttal by one of negative speakers.
6. Summation and rebuttal by one of affirmative speakers.

This form lends itself to many variations. Three speakers, rather than two, may be used on a team. The speeches may be of any convenient length. One speaker may open and close the case for his side, and the other conduct all the cross-examining.

The examiner must plan his series of short, pointed questions to expose weaknesses in the opponent's argument. Obviously, participation in cross-examination debate requires thorough preparation and special study of the questioning procedure. One of its special values is that it forces the debater to *know* his evidence, analysis, and argument. It keeps him from relying completely on a speech prepared in advance.

DIRECT-CLASH DEBATE

In direct-clash debate—originated in North Carolina by E. H. Paget—the debaters, after short opening speeches from each side to point up main areas of disagreement (clash), give a series of short speeches designed to establish or disprove one specific argument. It works like this:

1. The affirmative defines terms, analyzes the problem, and presents its case (usually five to eight minutes).
2. The negative agrees or disagrees with the affirmative analysis and gives its position on the proposition.
3. a. The affirmative then, in a short speech (usually three

minutes), presents one limited assertion and attempts to support it. For example, in a debate on the general proposition that the President of the United States should be elected by direct vote, the affirmative might offer as the first clash the contention: "The present electoral college system does not allow the people to elect a President favored by the majority."

   b. A negative speaker replies (usually for two minutes), attempting to counter this particular argument.

   c. Responses continue from speakers from the affirmative and negative alternately for four more speeches.

   d. The judge(s) award to one side a victory on this first clash.

4. The negative may now initiate the second clash. Alternately, the two sides debate this argument and the judges award a decision on the clash, as in 3 above.

The debate proceeds until one side has been awarded decisions in a certain number of clashes (usually three).

PROBLEM-SOLVING DEBATE

This type of debate, first used at the University of Washington, is a combination of discussion and debate. There are two teams of three speakers. The teams are not "affirmative" and "negative" teams. The problem is stated as a question. The debate proceeds in this manner:

1. *Analysis*
   a. The first speaker for team 1 analyzes the problem.
   b. The first speaker for team 2 presents his analysis of the problem.
2. *Solution*
   a. The second speaker for team 1 gives his proposal for solving the problem.

    b. The second speaker for team 2 proposes his solution
       to the problem.
3. *Evaluation*
    a. The third speaker for team 1 evaluates the analysis
       and solutions of any or all the preceding four speakers.
       He may praise the work of team 2 and criticize his
       colleagues if he wishes.
    b. The third speaker for team 2 evaluates what has been
       said by previous speakers.

If there is to be a decision on the debate, the judgment
consists of deciding which of the first speakers presented
the better analysis, which of the second speakers more adequately supported his solution, and which of the third
speakers gave the better evaluation.

EXERCISES

1. Write a report in which you discuss the similarities of, and differences between, a traditional debate and a courtroom trial.
2. Compare parliamentary debate with the forms of public discussion described in Chapter 5.
3. Suggest the ways in which so-called problem-solving debate is like discussion.

11

Preparing for Debate

The suggestions presented here will be aimed primarily at traditional debate, although the materials on preparation, rebuttal, and presentation have general applicability to all forms of debating.

The debater's preparation involves at least seven vital steps: (1) analyzing the problem; (2) finding evidence; (3) making a brief; (4) constructing a case; (5) tentatively organizing a constructive speech; (6) planning for refutation and rebuttal; and (7) rehearsing. The first five of these stages will be discussed in this chapter, the sixth in Chapter 12, and the seventh in Chapter 13.

ANALYSIS

What has been said about analysis in preparing for discussion (see Chapter 6) might well be repeated here. The process of analyzing requires investigation and explanation, not argument. Its purposes are to:

1. Explain the importance of the problem.
2. Discover the background and historical origins.
3. Define the language in which the problem is stated.

4. Discover the main points of controversy in order to determine the key issues.

From a written analysis, the reader should not be able to tell whether the writer is for or against the proposition. Writing the analysis, however, should help the writer decide what he feels should be done. More specifically, analysis helps the debater decide whether he wants to argue affirmatively or negatively.

Steps in analysis

A written analysis may contain seven distinct sections:

I. What is the immediate cause for the discussion? Why is the problem important now?

II. What is the history of the problem? Has this been a problem before now? What are the origins and historical development of the problem?

III. How should the terms of the stated proposition be defined?

IV. What arguments should be considered irrelevant to the controversy?

V. What arguments will be admitted and waived by both sides?

VI. What are the main arguments advanced by those for, and those against, the proposition?

VII. What are the main issues?

Some of these items require further explanation. For step three, definition of terms, the debater should understand methods of defining. A general procedure in making meaning clear is to (a) identify the generic class to which the term belongs; and (b) differentiate the particular term from all other members of the generic class. We can illustrate this method by defining a *square:* general class— a four-sided plane figure; differentiation—with equal sides and four right angles. To define most complex concepts, the debater will need to go beyond this dictionary method and employ some of the special methods of definition. These are:

1. Operational definition: tell how it works.
2. Negation: tell what it is not.
3. Etymology: give the derivation of the word.
4. Comparison and contrast: relate to something more familiar.
5. History: tell how concept developed historically.
6. Enumeration of details.
7. Authority: tell how "experts" have defined it.

Irrelevant matter is that which both sides agree has no bearing on the controversy. In debating whether the treaty-making powers of the President should be restricted, the speakers may consider irrelevant the argument that the President in practice does not now negotiate a treaty, and that negotiations are actually handled by the Secretary of State.

One issue which is almost always *waived* in debate is constitutionality. A decision to elect the President by direct vote of the people would require an amendment to the Constitution. When debating direct election, both sides usually ignore the argument that this proposal is now unconstitutional. The proposition says we *should* elect the President by direct vote; if this *ought to be* our policy, and if enough people in enough states think this policy is in the best interests of the nation, we can change the Constitution.

Step VI in the analysis may be helpful because it has the debater line up the main contentions of both sides. From these conflicting arguments, he should be able to see the main issues called for in step VII. Discovering the issues is the ultimate purpose of analysis.

Issues are those questions which indicate the disagreements, clashes, or controversies between those for and against the proposition. They should be worded so that the affirmative answers, "yes," and the negative, "no." If these key questions can be answered, the controversy will be settled.

Suppose you want to attend a movie and your parents object. The proposition is, Resolved: That you should attend motion picture X. You say: this movie is worth seeing. Your parents say: this movie is *not* worth seeing. Here we have a direct disagreement. The issue is evident: "Is motion pictureX worth seeing?" To this question, you on the affirmative answer, "yes," while your parents say, "no." Two other issues may arise: "Do you have enough money left from your allowance to pay the admission?" "Can you return home before eleven o'clock?" These three issues will determine the arguments for this "debate." If these three questions can be answered, either yes or no, the controversy will be ended.

Stock issues

In looking for the main issues in a proposition of policy, you will discover there are certain questions which appear in almost every problem. These common questions are referred to as *stock issues:*

1. Is there a need for a change from the present system? We presume the present system is satisfactory; before we are willing to change it, proponents of change (the affirmative) must show there are enough *evils* in the present system to warrant abandoning it. We must ask also if these evils are due to inherent weaknesses in the present system; perhaps the evils can be eliminated without changing the system.

2. Is the proposed change practicable; i.e., will it work? Will it remove the alleged evils?

3. Will the advantages accruing from the proposed change outweigh the disadvantages? Is the change desirable? The negative usually argues that the proposal will create more new evils than it eliminates from the present system.

4. Is the proposed change the best possible solution to the problem?

With these stock issues as a general guide, the debater who has made a careful analysis of a proposition can usually work out the specific controversies in a particular situation. The main contentions in a debate case come directly from the main issues.

FINDING EVIDENCE

The importance of systematic and thorough research has already been stressed (see Chapter 3). The debater who has not dug out the evidence—who may be heard to say, "Oh, *I* want to argue on the basis of 'pure' logic"—will be as conspicuous as an August snowman.

Start at once an ever-expanding bibliography of sources, and a note or card file of information on the problem. Exchange items with your colleagues. Read endlessly, discuss the problem with anyone who will listen, and strive constantly to clarify your lines of thought in making your position reasonable. The search for evidence should go on at all stages of preparation and participation. The debater may find it necessary to seek information before he becomes capable of analyzing the problem.

MAKING A BRIEF

Debaters often joke about the name of the document we are about to discuss, since it is anything but "brief." A brief is the *whole* argument on both sides, outlined in great detail, complete with support and references to the sources where the factual information was obtained. It can be thought of as the debater's storehouse of material. From it, he can organize several different constructive and rebuttal speeches which will vary according to the particular arguments selected for a specific occasion and the responses of the opposition.

The brief will be long and detailed if it is to contain everything the speaker can find out about the subject. Also, the brief should never stop growing. As long as the debater works with the problem, he should keep adding to and revising his brief.

The brief has three sections: introduction, body, and conclusion.

1. *The introduction.* This part contains the analysis prepared earlier. It is explanatory, not argumentative, and includes: (a) immediate cause for discussion; (b) history and origin of the problem; (c) definition of terms; (d) irrelevant matter; (e) admitted and waived matter; and (f) the main issues.

2. *The body.* The main section of the brief is a logical

outline of the arguments, the evidence which supports the
arguments, and the sources of factual information. If the
first main issue listed in the analysis is: "Is a change necessary?" the first argument in the body of the brief (in the
section giving the position of the affirmative) is: "A change
is necessary." This assertion is followed by the word "for"
and every statement following and subordinate to this
assertion is designed to support or prove it. Symbols of
I, A, l, a, etc., are used to indicate this subordinating relationship of statements. For example:

> I. A change to a policy of free trade for the U. S. is
>   necessary, for
>   A. Nations now friendly to the U. S. are being
>   forced to trade with communist nations, for
>   1. Western European nations are trading
>   with communist nations, for

U. S. News
Aug. 7, 1953

>   a. Britain is selling tin plate and chemi-
>   cals to communist nations
>   b. France is selling lead, iron, and steel
>   to communist nations
>   c. Denmark is selling oil tankers to com-
>   munist nations

*Business
Week,* April
10, 1954

>   2. In August, 1953, Argentina signed a
>   trade agreement with Russia to exchange
>   approximately $160 million worth of
>   goods.
>   3. . . . . .
>   B. . . . . .
> II. . . . . .

Notice the sources for the factual data on trade given in
the left-hand margin. References may be placed between

the lines of the brief or in footnotes at the bottom of each page.

Note also that the brief may be read either "down" or "up." Reading "down," the connecting word between statements is "because," or "for." Reading "up," the connecting word is "therefore." (France's imports exceeded exports in 1952; France's imports exceeded exports in 1953; etc. *Therefore,* France has an unfavorable import-export balance.)

It is vital that debaters see the logical relationship between assertion and support. Assertion must be followed by support; it invites support. Suppose there are ten of you in a room, and I say: "You are the oldest person in this room." If you respond, "How do you know?" or "Prove it," I must say: "You are the oldest person in this room, *because* (a) you are older than Frank; (b) you are older than Sue; (c) you are older than Mary; etc. I can prove each one of these supporting statements ("You are older than Frank, Sue, Mary, etc.) by bringing in your birth certificates and comparing them, by getting testimony from your mothers, from your doctors, etc. Reading "up" the logical chain, I would say: (a) You are older than Frank; (b) You are older than Sue; etc. *Therefore,* you are the oldest person in this room.

The body of the brief may also include sections of refutation. The argument expected from the opposition is stated, along with the counterargument, which is then supported in the subordinate statements. A brief of the affirmative position on a policy of free trade for the United States, for example, may contain a section such as the following:

> III. A policy of free trade can be initiated without serious disadvantages, for

A. Although the opponents of free trade argue
that the absence of a protective tariff would
endanger industries producing matériel for
national defense, national defense will be
maintained under a policy of free trade, for

1. The U. S. produces most of the strategic
goods required in the manufacture of defense matériel, for

Howard Piquet,   a. The U. S. produces 83% of the alumi-
Aid, Trade and   num used for domestic consumption.
the Tariff   b. The U. S. produces 90% of the optical
instruments used for domestic con-
sumption.

c. The U. S. produces about 93% of the
petroleum used for domestic consumption.

d.

e.

2.

B.

IV.

3. *The conclusion.* The conclusion of a brief is a summation of the arguments, together with a repetition of the
proposition. It may list all the main arguments advanced
in the body, starting each statement with the word "since."
"Since this is so, and this is so, and this is so, we hope you
will agree that we should adopt a policy of free trade."

A debater should work out a complete brief outlining
the position of both the affirmative and the negative so
that he becomes thoroughly familiar with the arguments
of the opposition. In a complete brief for both sides, the
order of sections is: (a) introduction; (b) position of the
affirmative; (c) summary (conclusion) of affirmative's posi-

tion; (d) position of the negative; and (e) summary of negative's position.

CONSTRUCTING A CASE

Up to this point, the debater has been working largely on his own. A brief drawn up by one person, if thorough, should look much like a brief on the same question compiled by another person. Also, the brief should contain *all* the possible arguments without regard to the problems of convincing a particular audience or meeting specific opponents.

The *case,* however, is an outline of particular arguments worked out by the members of an affirmative or negative team, and designed to convince a given audience. We are no longer working only with arguments on paper; we are ready to convince *people.*

You will first want to analyze the audience you are to address. Will it be large or small? Will the audience judge the debate or will an "expert" critic give the decision? Will the audience be predominantly young, middle-aged, or old? What will be the attitudes of listeners toward the proposition for debate? After asking and answering these kinds of questions, you will want to choose arguments and construct a case adapted to the interests and attitudes of this particular audience.

A second problem is deciding the most effective order in which to present your arguments. If most of the audience is against your side of the proposition, you may want to put first in your case the argument which is least controversial. Then you can gradually work into the arguments where you will meet resistance. If your audience is indifferent or undecided, you may want to begin your case with your most exciting and dramatic argument.

A minor task in working out the case is to divide the arguments in some logical fashion among the members of the team. If the need for change is the most controversial issue, and you have decided that this argument must come first in the case, you may have the first speaker deal with nothing except that one argument. The remainder of the case would then be developed by the other speaker or speakers.

The affirmative case

In debating a proposition of policy, the proponents of change are expected to assume what has been called the "burden of proof." They must produce evidence and reasoning sufficient to warrant giving up a system already in operation. If you can imagine a situation in which the negative had just exactly the same quantity and quality of evidence and reasoning as the affirmative, with all other factors being equal, then the negative position would triumph. This presumption in favor of what is working now puts a special burden on the affirmative.

To accept this challenge, the affirmative must present a complete case designed to convince a reasonable person that the change should be made (sometimes called a *prima facie* case). If you were advocating compulsory national health insurance, your case for a particular audience may sound something like this:

I. Millions of Americans are not receiving proper medical care today.

II. A majority of these millions cannot provide for their own medical protection through voluntary, private medical insurance.

III. Compulsory national health insurance can bring adequate medical care to all.

IV. This plan will not mean socialization of medicine or regimentation of doctors and patients.

Note particularly the relation of items I and II. Confusion often arises at the outset of an affirmative case in establishing need for a change. There are actually two levels at which the affirmative must operate:

1. General level: something is wrong in the present system. Conditions are unsatisfactory. There are many evils. (Not enough doctors, nurses, hospital beds; many persons denied medical care, etc.) There is a need for *some* kind of change.
2. Specific level: there is a need for compulsory national health insurance. The evils cannot be eliminated under the present system. People cannot provide for their own medical protection through present voluntary, private medical insurance.

The third assertion in the case suggested above is that this specific proposal will remedy the situation; and the fourth, that this remedy will not introduce worse evils than it eliminates.

Negative cases

A negative team has some choice in the kind of case it presents.

1. The negative can simply oppose. This approach is genuine negativism, and is sometimes called the "shotgun" negative: we'll shoot broadside at anything you propose. The weakness in this method, particularly in debates before audiences, is the failure to suggest what is to become of us if the affirmative establishes a need for changing the

present system. The speaker who does no more than oppose seems to be arguing in a vacuum. Most audiences would like to know what the negative speakers believe in, as well as what they are against.

2. The negative can defend the present system *(status quo)*. Here the negative attempts to prove the alleged evils are not serious enough to warrant change. They may add that the proposal of the affirmative would not be an improvement.

3. They can recognize imperfections in the present system, but suggest that these can be remedied (sometimes called a "modified *status quo*" case). The negative argues the weaknesses are not inherent in the present system, but can be eliminated without adopting the change proposed.

4. The negative can agree with the affirmative that changes are needed and advance a proposal for change which will be better than the affirmative plan. This case is the well-known *counterplan* case. The negative must be willing to assume the burden of proving that its plan will eliminate the evils. In fact, once the negative offers a counterplan, the debate becomes a struggle between two essentially "affirmative" teams; the audience must decide which plan can more effectively improve the situation.

ORGANIZING THE CONSTRUCTIVE SPEECH

When the case is outlined and the arguments divided among the speakers, each debater can start thinking about the organization of his ten-minute constructive speech. He knows the part of the case he is responsible for and he should see the best order for arranging his arguments. A word of caution is necessary, however. The debater should never consider a debate speech organized in *final* form.

The organization is always tentative. The superior debater must be capable of reorganizing his constructive speech in his head *while walking from his chair to the platform.*

Organizational ability is not a matter of magic, as this statement may suggest. Once the debater sees clearly the main contentions he and his colleague must establish, he can modify the arrangement of a particular constructive speech in a hurry. What the speaker must do in the preparation stage is to plan the *basic structure* of his speech. For example, the second affirmative speaker for compulsory national health insurance, in the case already mentioned, may have two basic arguments:

   I. Compulsory national health insurance can bring adequate medical care to all.
  II. This plan will not mean socialization of medicine or regimentation of doctors and patients.

He can organize a speech with these two divisions, and develop detailed supporting argument and evidence. Later, in a particular debate, the first negative speaker may spend half his speech arguing that compulsory insurance means socialization and regimentation of medicine. The audience may be in sympathy with this view. As the second affirmative speaker rises, he may realize that he must counteract this argument immediately, or lose the audience. It will be a simple matter for him to reverse the order of his two major contentions, developing his second argument first. Thus, he can start right off by saying:

Ladies and gentlemen, my friend of the opposition seems concerned about socialization and regimentation of medicine. Let's take a closer look at this argument. Will compulsory national health insurance mean the end of freedom for doctors and patients? Of course not. Let me show . . .

He has adapted his remarks to the opposition and to the audience; he is about to refute an argument of the speaker just preceding him, which is always a desirable accomplishment early in any debate speech; and, most important of all, he is giving an argument carefully prepared in advance which he wanted to deliver anyway!

In the early stages of planning organization for the constructive speech, the debater may profit from considering the *general* structure of the four constructive speeches in a traditional debate. Notice the repetition of the assertion-evidence units: "first contention, support for first contention; second contention, support for second contention"; etc. These outlines are suggestive only; no two debates will follow the same pattern.

The first affirmative speaker should:

   I. Introduce the question for debate.
     A. Make appropriate introductory remarks.
     B. Introduce the problem (why important, etc.).
     C. State the proposition.
     D. Define terms of the question.
     E. Set up the entire affirmative case (*optional*).
  II. State his first reason for supporting the proposition.
     A. Offer evidence to substantiate his first contention.
     B. Restate his first contention.
 III. State his second reason.
     A. Offer support.
     B. Restate.
     etc.
(N). Summarize his reasons for advocating the proposition.

The first negative speaker should:

    I. Adapt his remarks to opposition and audience.
        A. Make appropriate introductory remarks.
        B. Agree or disagree with affirmative definition of terms.
        C. Analyze the contention of the first affirmative speaker.
        D. Make a transition to his own beliefs, by refuting arguments of the first affirmative, if possible.
    II. State his first reason for objection to the proposition.
        A. Support.
        B. Restate.
        etc.
  (N). Summarize.

The second affirmative speaker should:

    I. Adapt his remarks to opposition and audience.
        A. Make appropriate introductory remarks.
        B. Deal with negative objections, if any, to definition of terms.
        C. Review *quickly* what his colleague argued in connection with analysis of first negative speaker's remarks.
        D. Show how affirmative case will overcome the objections of the negative (refutation).
    II. State his first contention.
        A. Support.
        B. Restate.
        etc.
  (N). Summarize.

The second negative speaker should:

    I. Adapt his remarks to opposition and audience.
        A. Make appropriate introductory remarks.
        B. Deal with definition of terms, if necessary.

    C. Analyze whole affirmative case in relation to negative's objections.

    D. Show how affirmative case becomes unwise in light of negative's arguments (refutation).

    E. Transition to rest of negative's case.

II. State his first contention.

    A. Support.

    B. Restate.

    etc.

(N). Review and summarize.

EXERCISES

1. Write an analysis of a current debate proposition, developing in outline form each of the seven steps of analysis suggested in this chapter.
2. Illustrate each of seven special methods of definition.
3. Write a report in which you discuss the similarities of and the differences between:
   a. A brief and a speech outline
   b. A brief and a case
   c. A case and a speech outline.
4. Draw up a brief, a case, and a speech outline on a current proposition. Show how these three structures are interrelated.

12

Refutation and Rebuttal

Debate by its nature involves controversy and opposition. Those who oppose deny, disagree, contradict, and try to disprove. Those attacked defend, bolster, and try to re-establish their position. These are the processes of *rebuttal;* each side: (1) *refutes*—questions, attacks, and disproves the arguments of opponents; and (2) rebuilds its own case after it has been assaulted—answers the questions, defends the arguments, and shows the audience that its position is still sound despite the attacks of the opposition.[1]

The debater who brushes aside lightly his preparation for rebuttal misunderstands the very essence of debate. If opposing speakers presented only their conflicting versions of the situation, without taking notice of the basic conflicts involved, the effect on the audience would be wholly

---

[1] This writer deplores the necessity of using military terms to characterize the advocacy stage of deliberation: attack, assault, defend, position. The words are reasonably apt; however, the metaphor is not a very good one because the relationship of affirmative and negative is not much like the relationship of attacker and defender on the battlefield. Opposing advocates share the same problem and are working toward the same goal; for the moment they disagree and are debating. Military enemies often have no common denominator for understanding except force, violence, and brutality.

unrealistic. The listener would be helped little, if at all, in deciding which course of action he favors. Opposing arguments must be scrutinized, the clash must be recognized, the evidence must be carefully examined and reexamined, and, finally, the debater must make clear to the listener the basis on which he must choose the affirmative or the negative position.

Skill in rebuttal can be increased by diligent preparation and practice. First, the ideal goal would be to know everything there is to know about the problem. If the speaker has examined all the evidence and every argument on both sides of the question, he will be ready for rebuttal. Second, the debater must practice. He must train himself to *see* clashes. He must learn to follow during a debate the pattern of essential disagreement which is unfolding. He must practice pointing out the weaknesses in opposing arguments, defending his own ideas, and reconstructing his case.

REFUTATION METHODS

General methods of refutation include exposing weaknesses in opposing arguments, exposing irrelevancies, showing inconsistencies in the opposition's position, and pointing out errors in the use of evidence and reasoning (fallacies). The debater should apply the tests of argument from specific instances, analogy, causal relation, etc. (see Chapter 4). Any deficiencies present may form the basis for refutation. In addition, of course, the rebuttal speaker offers counterargument; i.e., he disagrees with opposing arguments and attempts to present evidence which will show that his position is sounder than that of his opponent.

To dispute an opponent's ideas successfully, you must

have *evidence*. Refutation must be more than denial. It is not enough just to say: "The negative says we do not need a change but we of the affirmative have shown you in our constructive speeches that we do." In the rebuttal, you must present *evidence* that we need a change. It is true you have already presented some evidence of this need but the superior debater will have some *more* support to present in rebuttal; in addition, perhaps, he may repeat some of that presented earlier. What is more, he will use evidence which bears particularly and specifically on the points in controversy.

There are also some special methods of refutation which the debater should be able to use and recognize:

1. *Reductio ad absurdum.* In "reducing to absurdity," the speaker pretends to accept the argument of the opposition, but applies it in such extreme cases that it appears ridiculous. A common answer to proponents of welfare state measures (national health insurance, increased old-age security, etc.) is to argue: "If you want complete security guaranteed by the state, then the thing to do is go to jail; in prison you would have the ideal welfare state—guaranteed food, guaranteed housing, and absolute security in your old age." The audience may be impressed with *reductio ad absurdum* if they agree that the welfare state and prison are analogous situations. The other side will usually call the reduction to absurdity an unfair extension of their argument.

2. *The dilemma.* This method consists of calling attention to two or more possible courses of action, none of which the opposition can accept without damage to its case. The alternative possibilities are referred to as "horns" of the dilemma. The opponents of compulsory national

health insurance may argue: if this medical plan is adopted, doctors may (1) increase their patient load in order to make more money, which will lower the quality of medical care; (2) keep their present patient load, which will mean that medical care under this plan will be just what it is now, and which suggests there is no reason for changing from the present system; or (3) reduce their patient load because of lessened incentive, which will mean disastrous deterioration in present medical standards. At first glance, a dilemma like this one seems impressive and sometimes even escape-proof. In the short space of time encompassed by a debate, the good speaker must be able to find the weaknesses which almost always exist. Usually there will be possible courses of action other than the ones given. Another weakness may be that the consequences alleged will be unlikely, or not so damaging to the case as the opposition claims. In the third possibility listed in this example, for instance, medical deterioration would not result from reduced patient load if the number of practicing doctors were increased under the plan.

3. *Method of residues.* In this form of refutation, the debater lists the possible courses of action, and shows one by one why each is unsatisfactory except the final one. The weaknesses of this method are similar to those of the dilemma. The alternatives listed must exhaust the possibilities, and the reasons for rejecting each course and accepting the favored one must be sound.

4. *Turning the tables.* One of the most effective methods of refutation is that of "turning the tables," or using the opposition's arguments or evidence against them. The opportunity for doing so does not occur often but when it does the good debater will recognize it. In a debate on

compulsory national health insurance, the affirmative gave figures on the shortage of doctors to show the need for a change from the present system of medicine. The shortage they attributed to control by medical associations and medical schools of the numbers of students allowed to study for the profession. At the same time they maintained that doctors would still be free agents under their plan. The negative in trying to prove that this proposal would not improve medicine used the affirmative's figures and accepted the causes cited for the doctor shortage, arguing that medical cooperation in producing more doctors would be even less under compulsory health insurance.

REFUTATION IN CONSTRUCTIVE SPEECHES

The beginning debater inevitably asks: Should I refute the opposition during my constructive speech? If so, how much time can I devote to it? Should refutation come first or last or be scattered throughout the speech? No two debates are alike, of course, but in general good debaters do include refutation in their constructive speeches. Usually, they adapt to the remarks of the opposing speaker who has just left the floor, and answer early in their speech at least some of the more pressing points he has made. They do not allow their zeal in refuting to obscure the essentially constructive aspects of their speech. While developing their part of the case, they will take note of major disagreement heard from the opposition and offer abbreviated refutation in passing. They see to it that most of their time is devoted to constructive argument. The negative, of course, will be able to include more refutation in the constructive speeches than will the affirmative speakers.

THE REBUTTAL SPEECH

The rebuttal speech in traditional debate guarantees the speaker an opportunity to refute the opposing case and to defend his own. Since the time is provided for this purpose, it is not considered fair to use the rebuttal speech for introducing new arguments. However, the debater should not confuse the rule against presenting new arguments in rebuttal with offering new *evidence*. Additional evidence is an essential of successful rebuttal speeches.

The next most important component is careful organization. Too often the debater, in trying to answer each point made by the opposition, will attempt to take them up one by one just as he copied them in his notes. Such refutation will not be clear to the audience. There is never time enough to wade through such a "grocery list" of items. The debater is forced to stop when his time is up, leaving behind him a litter of unanswered pieces of arguments. The impression given to the listener is that he had few effective answers since he left much undone.

The rebuttal speaker, in the time available to him, must choose those arguments which most need answering, weeding out the trivial details. Then he must work out some kind of organization for his speech which will make his major contentions stand out emphatically.

One effective structure is to follow the outline of the clashes in the debate up to that point. For example, suppose the affirmative has offered the standard arguments that a change is necessary, that their plan will be the best change to make, and that their plan will work. Suppose the negative has challenged these arguments without present-

ing a counterplan. The affirmative might organize their
rebuttal speeches in this one, two, three order:

   I. We have told you a change is necessary; the negative has
       objected for these reasons: (1), (2), (3), but these objec-
       tions are not sound, because
       A.
          1.
          2.
       B.
          1.
          2.
  II. We contend this change is the best one we could make;
       the negative disputes this for these reasons: (1), (2), (3),
       but their arguments are not acceptable, because
       A.
          1.
          2.
       etc.
 III. etc.

Each affirmative speaker may be able to use this same general structure. The second speaker should then include in
his refutation whatever new objections the negative rebuttal speaker has added on each of these main contentions.

The negative rebuttal speakers in this same debate
could also use this organization if they chose. They would
say the affirmative speakers have based their case on three
main assertions. They then would attack them one by one.
This procedure is quite different from the "grocery list"
structure since here the speaker is dealing with the major
clashes in the debate.

Another outline would be used when the negative offers
a counterplan. The affirmative might say:

I. The plan of the negative will not solve our problems, because
   A.
      1.
      2.
   B.
   etc.
II. Our plan does not have the same weaknesses as the negative plan, because
   A.
   B.
   C.

The negative speakers may simply reverse this organization.

There is no intent here to suggest these outlines as "canned" formulae for the rebuttal speech. There are many possible ways of structuring a successful effort. These examples are given to suggest ways in which the debater may invent patterns for grouping his rebuttal. Whatever structure is used, the rebuttal speech must be clearly organized if it is to be effective. It must cover the main points of disagreement (clashes), and it must not become a jumbled mass of disconnected detail.

EXERCISES

1. Locate printed verbatim reports of several debates (in *University Debaters' Annual,* or a similar source). Find examples of the general methods of refutation and of *reductio ad absurdum,* dilemma, method of residues, and turning the tables.

2. Listen to a traditional debate. Attempt to outline the rebuttal speeches as you hear them. Then write a report in which you describe and evaluate the organization of each rebuttal speech.

13

Presentation

Debaters often need to be reminded that they are public speakers. Sounds incredible, doesn't it? Yet, you can hear debates which only faintly resemble *public* performances. When speakers use a jargon incomprehensible except to other debaters, talk at a rate much too rapid for comfortable intelligibility, and dodge responsibility for explaining concepts clearly because "the opposition and the judge have heard these arguments before and know what we mean," they ignore the function of the public speaker. They seem to assume they are engaging in some kind of special activity where the sensible requirements of good speaking don't apply.

The debater must *communicate* his ideas. Otherwise, he is wasting his time and the time of his listeners. The standards of good public speaking must be applied to debate. When a debater is guilty of poor public speaking, he is the perpetrator of poor debating.

REHEARSAL

A wise speaker will rehearse any public speech before he attempts to deliver it. Although individuals vary in the rehearsal methods they prefer, the following suggestions may be helpful.

1. Don't rehearse until you are thoroughly prepared,

until you have sufficient evidence at your finger tips, and until your tentative outline is written in concrete form. The purpose of practice is not to exercise the voice; you do that many hours each day. You want to practice express-ing *ideas* in understandable *language*. You can't express ideas until you have examined carefully the factual ma-terials which tend to support them. Only after you have ironed out the wrinkles of organization and support are you ready to rehearse. You wouldn't polish an automobile until after you had washed off the mud!

2. Speak from the outline during rehearsal. At this stage, you can become familiar with the ordering of your ideas. During an actual debate, you will hope to take only an occasional peek at your outline. Certainly you do not want to write out the speech in manuscript form and attempt to practice from manuscript. Good debating requires constant and immediate adaptation and completely extem-poraneous speaking. By diligent practice in speaking from outlines, you can develop the extemporaneous skills debate demands.

3. If possible, persuade a friend to listen to one of your final rehearsals. Ask him to feed back to you some of the ideas you are trying to communicate. If you are not getting your thoughts through to him, you must redouble your efforts.

4. You may want to word carefully and memorize key opening, transitional or closing sentences, main arguments, and the like. Develop such a procedure cautiously, how-ever. You should not memorize long passages. Quotations and involved statistical tables should be typed on cards. When speaking, pick up the card and read from it. One debater I worked with had a phenomenal memory. He

could remember long lists of figures. But audiences were never convinced; they thought he must be making them up as he needed them. Critics would invariably comment: "Seems to be talking too much 'off the cuff.'"

DELIVERY

The big moment for a debater is the actual delivery of his constructive and rebuttal speeches. The weeks of reading and investigating, briefing and case-making, outlining and rehearsing, all culminate in the speech presentation. What a pity it is to watch a well-informed and thoroughly prepared debater throw away any claim to distinction through ineffective delivery! Resolve to make the most of every speaking opportunity by making your delivery the very best.

Language

The debater shares with the discusser the problems of language accuracy and preciseness (see Chapter 7). You must practice making your ideas clear through careful language usage. The debater must avoid debate jargon. He should not try to convey meaning with words which express only part of an idea.

1. Avoid triteness: "my colleague"; "my partner"; "honorable judge"; "worthy opponents"; "we of the negation"; etc. Think of fresh symbols for these meanings.

2. Avoid words which refer to ideas which are meaningful to you and the opposing debaters, but meaningless to an audience not familiar with debate jargon: "We have outlined our need"; We have established need, practicability, and a plan"; etc. In a debate on federal legislation to insure fair employment practices, a speaker said: "If

your broad need exists in the South, how are you going to meet your need?" *Translation:* "If the greatest problems of discrimination in employment exist in the South, and if the South shows the greatest resistance to federal legislation, how will the affirmative proposal for federal legislation eliminate discrimination?" Notice we must substitute for the jargon terms concrete words describing this specific problem of discrimination. Later the speaker said: "The *status quo* is inherently incapable of dealing with the present system." But the *status quo is* the present system. The "translation" of this sentence is ridiculous: "The present system is inherently incapable of dealing with the present system."

3. Avoid exaggerated language: "We have proved beyond a doubt"; "We have proved conclusively"; "Any reasonable person will concur with us that . . ."; etc.

4. Avoid vague references which may mean that you are not actually referring to anything concrete: "statistics prove . . ."; "authoritative opinion is that . . ."; "it has been shown that . . ."; "everyone knows . . ."; etc. If statistics prove it, cite the figures, and give the source where they can be examined.

Voice

Audiences do not demand that you have a "cultivated," "melodious," or "beautiful" voice. They do expect two things: (1) to understand you; and (2) to be able to listen to you throughout your whole speech without strain, pain, or falling asleep. Let's review your responsibilities for achieving the first requirement, understandability:

1. Speak with enough volume and force to be heard. At the same time, be natural. Sound much as you would in

conversation. Be yourself, not a pale imitation of a Senator.

2. Articulate the sounds of each word distinctly. We Americans sometimes try to get by with cluttered and abbreviated sounds. We say: "gonna"; "gotta"; "Uni States of Merca"; etc. The danger here is that audiences will misunderstand your *meanings* because they missed a *word* or two. Of course, you should not go to the other extreme and make your articulation painfully precise. Just give your audience a fair break; don't make them guess what you mean.

3. Speak slowly enough to be understood. Among errors made by debaters, rapid-fire speaking is in a class by itself. They often try to crowd fifteen minutes of material into every ten-minute speech; then in rebuttal, where time is short and arguments to be answered numerous, they speak even faster. A machine-gun rate doesn't pay. It is more effective to develop two arguments at a sensible, understandable rate, than to race through three arguments at a pace so rapid the audience cannot follow you.

The second requirement for adequate voice usage is listenability; i.e., the audience must be able to listen to you without loss of interest. The principal suggestion here is to avoid monotony. The listener finds it difficult to respond steadily to a single stimulus for any length of time. To hold his attention, the speaker must avoid monotonous loudness and rate. We all have experienced the drowsiness which can result from a speech delivered in a monotone, at a fixed loudness level, and an unchanging pace. Meaningful changes in volume should occur frequently. Some ideas are more important than others and deserve more emphasis. Key concepts may be emphasized also by reducing the loudness level. Rate, too, should be varied. Main arguments, complex causal relationships, involved statistical computations, and the like, should be presented more slowly than other parts of the speech. Pauses between main divisions should be longer than between sentences within a division.

Just in case we may be misunderstood, let's add here that voice alone, obviously, cannot make you worth listening to, no matter how skillfully it is manipulated. You must also be saying something worth while.

Bodily action

Your listenability rating will be helped also by effective use of movement, posture, gesture, eye contact, and facial expression. Action should contribute to the communication of ideas; it should not call attention to itself. The speaker should be animated. He should face the audience directly, look them squarely in the eyes, and show by his facial expression that he believes sincerely what he is saying and wants his audience to listen to him. Movement, gesture, and other aspects of bodily action deserve careful thought and diligent practice.

ADAPTATION

Everything the speaker does should be appropriate to the situation. He should always dress neatly, but whether he wears coat and tie will depend on the formality of the occasion. Speaking in a large hall obviously requires greater volume and more vigorous gestures. In his opening remarks, the debater should take note of the occasion; invariably he should make appropriate introductory remarks.

The debater must adapt his remarks to the particular audience he is addressing. Examples used, simplicity of explanations, and such factors should vary with the age, occupation, level of understanding, and attitudes of listeners.

The manner of greeting the audience is a minor problem which seems to worry most debaters. It is now old-fashioned to use what once was a standard opening: "Mr. Chairman, Worthy Opponents, Honorable Judges." The best greeting is the simplest greeting. Usually there is a chairman, and he should always be addressed, since he is recognizing the speaker and assigning him the right to the floor. If there are only a few persons in the audience, the simple word, "Friends," would be appropriate. If you have a fair gathering of men and women, or a large crowd, the simplest acceptable greeting is, "Ladies and Gentlemen." Your opening would then be: "Mr. Chairman, Ladies and Gentlemen."

ATTITUDE

An audience expects the debater to be courteous and polite to the opposition and to everyone else in the room. Your conduct before, during, and even after the debate will influence audience judgment of you as a speaker. Some participants before a debate appear smug, and cast deprecating glances at the opposition which seem to say: "This one is going to be easy." During the debate, while a member of the opposition is speaking, debaters have been known to confer constantly, hold an audible conversation, grin indulgently as if the speaker were a complete idiot, and in other ways ignore what the opposition is saying. Make no mistake about it: this kind of discourtesy will brand you as a person who is not really interested in deliberating intelligently about an important public problem. Even after the debate is over, audiences will be disappointed in you if you are flippant about the critic's suggestions for improvement, or rude to the opposition.

The speakers who happen to be opposing you are not stupid. They are just as intelligent, just as sincere, and just as competent to debate this proposition as you are. Even if they are not, society expects you to pretend they are! We meet together to give each side a fair hearing. It is inconsiderate to be sarcastic about the preparation, abilities, or attitudes of the opposition. Sarcasm is an easy weapon to use, and at first it seems like great sport to the user. A debater once said to a team of girls from the University of Illinois: "We always thought the University of Illinois offered courses in political science; but apparently it doesn't because these girls don't seem to know any of the simple fundamentals of political science. As debaters, we think these girls ought to stick to being mothers." In this case, the judge filled out his ballot and left the room before the debate was over! Sarcasm has no place in intelligent deliberation.

EXERCISES

1. Listen to an interschool debate. Make a list of the trite expressions and the jargon terms used.
2. After listening to a debate, write a report in which you evaluate the delivery of the speakers.

14

Evaluating Debate

What was said about judging discussion (see Chapter 6) must be repeated here. Deliberation is evaluated according to its *outcomes,* not by the techniques employed. Debate on the floor of Congress or in the courtroom is judged on the *merits of the question.* That is, we ask: Shall we adopt this proposed plan or not? Is the defendant guilty or innocent?

An audience may be asked to vote after a debate on the policy they favor. One popular form of ballot is the shift-of-opinion ballot. The listeners record before the debate whether they are for, against, or undecided. After the debate, each person votes again. He is given an opportunity on the ballot to show he is even more strongly for or against the proposition than he was before. Analysis of the ballots will then show how the audience shifted as a result of the debate.

We are also interested in those who are *learning* the *procedures* of debate. Our immediate evaluation concerns the merits of the debating.

Criteria

The debater is usually judged as an individual speaker on criteria like these:

1. Content
   a. Understanding of subject
   b. Definition of terms
   c. Clear analysis
   d. Sound reasoning
   e. Substantial, accurate, specific, and convincing evidence.
2. Organization of speeches
3. Refutation and rebuttal
   a. Adaptation to opposing case
   b. Summary of opposing argument
   c. Effectiveness of refutation and counterarguments
   d. Rebuilding of case.
4. Delivery
   a. Fluency
   b. Effective use of language
   c. Adaptation to audience and situation
   d. Effective use of voice
   e. Effective bodily action.

Some ballots also include items on debate manners, such as punctuality, respect for time limits, serious attitude toward the debate, courtesy toward opponents, critics, and audience and willingness to listen to opposition arguments.

Team ratings are often given along with individual speaker evaluation. Additional factors being judged here are such things as the quality of the whole case as presented by both speakers, their consistency with each other, and their smoothness as a functioning unit.

Rating scales

Reports filled out by debate critics contain one or more of the following judgments:

1. A quality rating of each individual debater. The judge may be asked to assign to each debater a rating of superior, excellent, good, fair, etc.

2. An itemized rating of each debater on each of several criteria. On this type of ballot, the judge must assign, for each speaker, ratings such as these:

Analysis	4
Reasoning	5
Evidence	3
Rebuttal	5
Organization	2
Delivery	4

3. A *ranking* of the four debaters in a given debate. The best debater is ranked 1; the next best, 2; the third best, 3; and the poorest, 4. Notice that each debater might be *rated* superior, or 5, but if rankings are asked for, one of the superior debaters must still be fourth best in the debate.

4. A quality rating for each team.

5. A *decision*—a judgment as to which team, affirmative or negative, did the better debating.

An example of a rating scale is the following:

DEBATE EVALUATION REPORT

Evaluate each speaker for quality of debating performance on a five-point scale: 5—Superior; 4—Excellent; 3—Good; 2—Below Average; 1—Poor. For uniformity in judgment, judges are asked to consider the elements of debate listed below; it is NOT NECESSARY to give a separate rating for each element or to consider elements of equal weight. Assign a single rating for each speaker.

Content		Rating
Knowledge		
Analysis	1st Affirmative	....
Reasoning		
Evidence	2nd Affirmative	....
Organization		
Refutation and Rebuttal	1st Negative	....
Adaptation		
Delivery	2nd Negative	....
Clear and effective		
communication of ideas		

TEAM RATING: Evaluate each team for quality of debating, using the five-point scale above.

Convincingness of total argument		Rating
Consistency		
Attitude, Courtesy	Affirmative Team	....
	Negative	....

DECISION: In my opinion, the better debating was done by the..team.

SUGGESTIONS FOR IMPROVEMENT

1st Affirmative	*1st Negative*
2nd Affirmative	*2nd Negative*

EXERCISES

1. Listen to a traditional debate and evaluate each speaker on a rating scale such as the one suggested in this chapter. Write a report in which you indicate your answers to such questions as the following:

   a. Does this rating scale allow the critic to evaluate accurately the success of the debaters?

   b. Which rating scale is better—one which asks for ratings on itemized criteria such as analysis, reasoning, organization, etc., or one which asks for an over-all rating for each debater?

2. Design rating scales for debaters participating in:

   a. Parliamentary debate

   b. Cross-examination debate

   c. Direct-clash debate

   d. Problem-solving debate.

15

Ethics in

Deliberation

Now that you have taken a look at the theory and pro
cedures involved in deliberation, you may be moved to
ask, "What is the point to all this training in discussion
and debate?" As we said in the first chapter, the techniques
of deliberation are vital because they are the processes involved in democratic decision-making. For you as an individual, moreover, such training should have additional
values. The long-range objectives of training in discussion
and debate are very similar to the over-all objectives of
education in general: learning to think, to analyze, to
evaluate evidence, to make judgments; learning to be articulate about problems; learning to get along with other
people. These abilities, in turn, make it easier to earn a
living and function as a citizen.

If you accept these objectives as your real goals, your
philosophy of participation requires rational, reasonable
deliberation for long-term success and not questionable,
expedient manipulation for temporary gain. The delibera
tor must be honest. You must reject unethical methods
even when they can win for you an immediate victory.

It is obvious that fabrication of evidence, inventing of

sources, and deliberate misquoting are dishonest. Some other violations of ethical standards are not so obvious. Sometimes it is difficult to tell when an authority has been quoted out of context or a source unfairly identified. To prove dishonesty, it would be necessary to establish intent; when a deliberator fails to explain that the authority being quoted has a bias, we cannot be sure the omission is intentional. Rather than try to identify the occasional cheat, it is more feasible to charge the sincere student with the responsibility for keeping his sights high and his hands clean, to mix the metaphor. If he has such goals as learning to think and becoming a good citizen, he will not stoop to immorality for selfish advantage.

The deliberator is learning to use powerful tools when he learns how groups reach decisions and how individuals and audiences are persuaded. He will be violating the trust of his teachers if he uses persuasion to mislead, to distort, or to deceive. If he has a sense of ethics, he will not leave out part of a quotation to make it sound more favorable than it really is; he will not mumble or rush through the identification of a source because it would really be an unfavorable reference if carefully identified; and he will not be guilty of any of the whole range of questionable practices which most discussers and debaters know so well.

The deliberator will give little to the democratic society of which he is privileged to be a part by studying the individual pieces of theory presented here if all is to be thrown away through deception and dishonesty. Instead, deliberation should contribute to the general welfare by bringing about wiser decisions. The participant who wants to be fair will follow the spirit and the letter of a code of ethics.

Index

Adaptation, to audience, 106, 129-130
to occasion, 129-131
Advocacy, 5-9
Affirmative case, 107-108
Agricultural Index, 24
All-inclusive language, 70
Alternative syllogism, 40-41
tests of, 47-48
Ambiguity, 14-15, 70
America's Town Meeting of the Air, 76
Analogy, 37-38
figurative, 37-38
literal, 37
tests of, 43
Analysis, 59, 97-101
defined, 59
stage in discussion, 62-63
steps in, 98
Appeal to authority, 48
to tradition, 49
Arguing in a circle, 49
Argument, defined, 31, 36
Argumentum ad hominem, 48
Argumentum ad verecundiam, 48
Articulation, 128
Attitude in debate, 130-131, 136
in discussion, 67-69, 86, 87
Audience adaptation, 106, 129-130
Authority, 38-39
of discussion leader, 81-83
of parliamentary chairman, 82
tests of, 44-45

Ballots, debate, 134-136
discussion, 85-87
Band wagon fallacy, 48

Begging the question, 49
Biographical dictionaries, 25
Bodily action, 129
Briefing, 102-106
Burden of proof, 15-16, 107-108

Case, 106-109
affirmative, 107-108
negative, 108-109
Categorical syllogism, 39-40
tests of, 45-46
Caucuses, 55
Causal relationship, 38
tests of, 44
Cause to effect, 38
Chicago Round Table, 76
Closed-group discussion, 52-56
Committee, 54
Committee of the whole, 55
Concrete language, 71
Congressional Record, 25
Connotation, 71
Consensus, 2
Counterplan case, 109
Cross-examination debate, 92-93

Debate, analysis, 97-101
briefing, 102-106
case, 106-109
defined, 9
ethics, 138-139
evaluation, 133-136
jargon, 126-127
organizing speeches, 109-113, 120-122
presentation, 124-131
proposition, 15-16
rating scales, 134-136

Debate, analysis—(*Continued*)
  refutation and rebuttal, 115-122
  research, 19-27, 101-102
  stock issues,100-101
  types of, 89-95
Deduction, 33, 36, 39-42
  tests of, 45-48
Definition, methods of, 98-99
  process, 70
  stage in discussion, 62
Deliberation, 1-7
  ethics, 138-139
Deliberation continuum, 3-8
Delivery, 126-129
Denotation, 71
Dewey, John, 62
Dictionary of American Biography, 25
Dictionary of National Biography, 25
Dilemma, 117-118
Direct-clash debate, 93-94
Direct evidence, 34
Discussion, analysis, 59
  attitude, 67-69
  defined, 8
  ethics, 138-139
  evaluation, 85-87
  leadership, 77-83
  outline, 61-64
  participation, 67-75
  physical arrangements, 64-65
  questions, 13-15
  rating scales, 85-87
  research, 19-27, 60
  synthesis, 60-61
  types of, 51-57
Dogmatism, 74
Duties of constructive speakers, 111-113
Duties of leader, 78-81

Education Index, 24
Effect to cause, 38
Effect to effect, 38
Emergence of problems, 1-3

Emotional thinking, 48-49
Encyclopedia of the Social Sciences, 25
Ending discussion, 80, 87
Enthusiasm in discussion, 74
Enthymeme, 42
Ethics in deliberation, 138-139
Evaluation, of debate, 133-136
  of discussion leader, 86-87
  of discussion outcome, 85
  of discussion performance, 86
  of sources, 26-27
Evidence, defined, 31-33
  direct, 34
  indirect, 34
  negative, 35
Exaggerated language, 127
Expert testimony, 35

Facts, defined, 33
Fallacies, 42-49
False cause, 44
Figurative analogy, 37-38
Forum, 57
Forum period, 80-81

Generalization, 36-39, 43
Goals, 63
Government publications, 25
Group outline, 61-64
Guiding discussion, 80, 87

Hasty generalization, 43
Hearsay, 35
History of the problem, 97-98
Honesty in deliberation, 138-139
Humor, 78
Hypothetical syllogism, 40
  tests of, 46-47

Illini Forensic Association, 91
Illinois, University of, 91
Impartiality of leader, 78, 81-83
Indirect evidence, 34

Induction, 33-36
  by analogy, 37-38
  by authority, 38-39
  by causal relation, 38
  by specific instances, 37
  tests of, 42-45
Inference, 30
Informality in discussion, 65
Information Please Almanac, 25
Intelligence of leader, 77
Interpersonal relations, 72-73
Interviewing, 23
Introducing discussion, 79-80, 87
Irrelevant matter, 99
Issues, 100-101

Jargon in debate, 126-127
Joint committee session, 55
Judging debate, 133-136
  discussion, 85-87

Knowledge, 77-78
  of discussion technique, 77-78
  of subject, 77-78

Language, in discussion, 69-72
  in debate, 126-127
Leader, authority of, 81-82
  as contributor, 81-83
  duties of, 78-81
Leadership qualities, 77-78
  impartiality, 78
  intelligence, 77
  knowledge, 77-78
  social sensitivity, 78
  speech skills, 78
Listenability, 128-129
Listening, 23
  in discussion, 73-74, 86
Literal analogy, 37
Legislative assembly, 53-55
  committee of, 54
  parliamentary assembly of, 54-55

Merits of debating, 133
Merits of the question, 133

Method of residues, 118
Modified *status quo* case, 109

Negative cases, 108-109
  counterplan, 109
  modified *status quo,* 109
  "shotgun," 108-109
  status quo, 109
Negative evidence, 35
New York Times, 24
New York Times Index, 24
Non causa pro causa, 44
Non sequitur, 43
Northwestern University Reviewing
    Stand, 76
Note-cards, 20-21
  classification of, 20
  identifying source, 20
Note-taking, 20-21

Objectivity, 67-69
  in language, 70
  obstacles to, 68-69
Observation, 22-23
  accuracy of, 22
  reporting accurately, 22
  reporting fairly, 22-23
Ordinary testimony, 35
Oregon, University of, 92
Organizing constructive speech, 109-
    113
Organizing the rebuttal, 120-122
Orthodox debate, 89-90
Outline, group, 61-64
  complete sentence, 60-61

Paget, E. H., 93
Pamphlet materials, 24
Panel, 53, 56-57
  problem-solving, 53
  public, 56-57
Parliamentary chairman, 82
Parliamentary debate, 90-92

Pattern, 61
Personal experience, as source, 21-22
Physical arrangements, 64-65
Planning discussion, 79
"Poisoning the well," 48
Policy determining discussion, 52-57
Post hoc, ergo propter hoc, 44
Power of group to act, 3-7
Probability, 29
Problem-solving debate, 94-95
Problem-solving panel, 53
Propositions, 12-15
  debatability of, 15
  of fact, 12-13
  of policy, 12
  of value, 12
  wording of, 15
Public Affairs Information Service, 24
Public discussion, 56-57
Purposes of analysis, 97-98
Purposes of discussion, 52

Question period, *see* Forum
Questions for discussion, 11-14
  appropriateness, 13
  impartiality, 14
  limitation, 13-14
  non-ambiguity, 13
  of fact, 11-12
  of policy, 11-12
  of value, 11-12

Rate of speaking, 127-129
Rating scales, for debate, 134-136
  for discussion, 85-87
Reader's Guide to Periodical Literature, 24
Reasoning, 31, 35-36
Rebuttal, defined, 115-116
Recommendation groups, 5-6, 8, 52-55
Reductio ad absurdum, 117

Refutation, 115-119
  defined, 115
  in constructive speech, 119
  methods of, 116-119
Regulating discussion, 80, 87
Rehearsal, 124-126
Reluctant witness, 45
Reporting observations, 22-23
  accuracy of, 22
  fairness of, 22-23
Robert's Rules of Order, 82, 92

Self-enlightenment, discussion for, 55-57
Shifting ground, 49
"Shotgun" negative case, 108-109
Solutions, in discussion, 63-64
Sources of evidence, 35
  expert testimony, 35
  hearsay, 35
  ordinary testimony, 35
Speaking, as leader, 78
  in debate, 124-131
  in discussion, 73, 86, 87
Specific instances, 37
  tests of, 43
Statesman's Yearbook, 25
Statistical Abstract of the U. S., 25
Statistical information, 25
Status quo negative case, 109
Stock issues, 100-101
Summarizing discussion, 80, 87
Support, 31
Syllogism, 39-41
  tests of, 45-48
Symposium, 57
Synthesis, defined, 60

Tact, in discussion, 74, 86
Testing sources, 26-27
  for accuracy, 26
  for completeness, 26
  for prejudice, 26
  for recency, 26

Town Meeting of the Air, 76
Traditional debate, 89-90
Triteness, 126
Turning the tables, 118-119

Understandability in speaking, 127-
    128

Vertical File Service, 24
Voice, 127-129

Waived matter, 99
Washington, University of, 94
Who's Who, 25
World Almanac, 25